WHEN
THE CROSSES
ARE GONE

WHEN THE CROSSES ARE GONE

RESTORING SANITY TO A WORLD GONE MAD

Michael Youssef, Ph.D.

DUNHAM
books

When the Crosses Are Gone © 2011 by Michael Youssef

Published in Nashville, Tennessee by Dunham Books. For information regarding special sales or licensing, please contact the publisher:

Dunham Books
63 Music Square East
Nashville, Tennessee 37203

ISBN 978-0-9837456-2-4

Printed in the United States of America

Table of Contents

"A great civilization is not conquered from without until it has destroyed itself from within."

—Will Durant

Chapter One

The Dangerous, Offensive Cross

A cross is a dangerous thing. In 1934, the Veterans of Foreign Wars put up a cross far out in the Mojave Desert, a memorial to soldiers killed in World War I. The seven-foot cross stood atop a stony outcropping called Sunset Rock. To get there, you had to leave Los Angeles and drive three and a half hours northeast on U.S. 15, past Victorville and Barstow, past Zzyzx Mineral Springs, then turn south onto Cima Road, a two-lane blacktop. You would then go almost nine miles into the Mojave National Preserve, and probably not see another human being along the road. Arriving at Sunset Rock, you would see no signs, no inscriptions, just a simple white cross which had stood undisturbed for almost eight decades.

In 2001, a former Park Service employee sued the government, demanding that the cross be removed. This began a nearly decade-long legal battle. A judge ordered that the upper portion of the cross be covered by a plywood box, so that it looked like a blank signboard instead of a cross. The case was battled all the way to the United States Supreme Court.

For some reason, a lonely cross out in the remoteness of the Mojave Desert was so threatening that a host of powerful organizations joined the campaign to destroy it. Those organizations included the American Humanist Association, Atheist Alliance International, the Freedom from Religion Foundation, Americans United for Separation of Church and State, People for The American Way, and the American Civil Liberties Union.

On April 28, 2010, the Supreme Court rendered a 5-4 decision, ruling that a cross in the middle of the desert did not undermine our constitutional republic. Writing for the majority, Justice Anthony Kennedy observed, "The goal of avoiding governmental endorsement [of religion] does not require eradication of all religious symbols in the public realm."[1] Less than two weeks later, around May 10 or 11, thieves went to Sunset Rock, cut the mounting bolts, and stole the cross. Today there is no cross on Sunset Rock.

Even in the Mojave Desert, where almost no one ever saw it, a cross is a dangerous thing. Those who felt threatened by it had to destroy it.

It has always been this way.

Exchanging Crosses For Red Stars

In November 1917, Vladimir Lenin and the Communists seized power in Russia during the bloody Bolshevik Revolution. There was no room for God under the new regime. The Communists invaded churches and carted away sacred objects and religious images. They eliminated religious holy days, such as Christmas and Easter, and replaced them with state-sanctioned festivals in honor of Marx and Lenin. They denounced the clergy as enemies of the Revolution, and then executed them.

Lenin's goal was to replace the Christian religion with a godless Communist religion. Those who once followed Jesus had to join the cult of Lenin. Churches became temples of devotion to the State. Hymns of praise to God were replaced by anthems praising the Revolution. All across Russia, soldiers climbed to the pinnacles of church buildings, tore down the cross, and replaced it with the red star of the new Soviet state.

Throughout the formerly Christian realm of Mother Russia, all the crosses were gone.

Years passed. Lenin died in 1924 and was replaced by the even more ruthless Joseph Stalin. At the end of World War II and with the defeat of Nazi Germany, the leaders of the Allied nations—President Harry S. Truman, Britain's Prime Minister Winston Churchill, and Soviet dictator Joseph Stalin—met in Potsdam, occupied Germany, to discuss how to establish order in the post-war world. At one point, Churchill warned Stalin that Pope

Pius XII would be displeased if the Communists took control of Poland, a predominantly Catholic nation. Stalin scornfully retorted, "Mr. Prime Minister, how many divisions did you say the Pope had?"[2]

Stalin proceeded to subjugate all of Eastern Europe—Bulgaria, Romania, Yugoslavia, Albania, Hungary, Czechoslovakia, Poland, and East Germany. Throughout these once-free, once-Christian nations, Communist soldiers tore down the crosses and replaced them with red stars. From the Baltic to the Adriatic to the Black Sea, all the crosses were gone.

Years passed. The people of Eastern Europe suffered under the tyranny of godless Communism.

Then, in June 1979, Pope John Paul II made a nine-day pilgrimage to his homeland, Poland. Just as Stalin had said decades earlier, the Pope came without armies. He came in peace. Yet the Communist authorities who ruled over Poland feared him. They were afraid to let him come—yet they were even more afraid of what might happen if they tried to stop him. The Pope threatened the Communists, because they associated him with the cross.

And the cross is a dangerous thing.

From the moment Pope John Paul II kissed the ground at Warsaw airport, the Communists did everything they could to downplay the Pope's visit. For example, Polish state television had a commentator chatter over the Pope's message. Yet nearly a third of the population of Poland turned out to see the Pope, and the rest of the people watched on television.

By coming to Poland in the name of the cross, Pope John Paul II changed the course of history. Three years later, the Pope received President Ronald Reagan in the Papal Library at the Vatican. Both men had survived recent assassination attempts. As they talked together, the American president told the Polish pope that he believed God had spared their lives in order to bring down the godless Communist system. "Hope remains in Poland," Ronald Reagan said. "We, working together, can keep it alive."[3]

In June 1989—ten years after Pope John Paul II's triumph in pilgrimage to Poland in the name of the cross—the government of Poland permitted elections in which non-Communist candidates campaigned for election. Candidates from the non-Communist Solidarity union won a majority of seats. For the first time since the end of World War II, Poland had a non-Communist government.

Two years later, the Soviet Union collapsed. All across Eastern Europe and Russia, the red stars came down. The crosses came back.

Today there are crosses in Eastern Europe. There is faith in Eastern Europe. But in America, where religious freedom is guaranteed by the First Amendment to the Constitution, the cross is considered a dangerous thing. Even a cross out in the middle of the desert poses a threat.

Editing Out The Cross

Even in the hands of an eleven-year-old girl, a cross is a dangerous thing.

Kandice Smith, a sixth-grader at Curry Middle School in Walker County, Alabama, was excited to receive a cross necklace as a gift from her parents. She wore it to school as a quiet symbol of her Christian faith. But when school officials saw it, they ordered her to hide it inside her blouse. Even though the school's dress code policy stated that accommodation should be made for a student's religious beliefs, officials claimed the rule against neck jewelry was designed to prevent "gang activity."

Threatened with suspension, Kandice insisted on her right to display the cross necklace under both school rules and the U.S. Constitution. The American Center for Law and Justice filed suit in U.S. District Court on Kandice Smith's behalf. Stuart J. Roth, counsel for the ACLJ, said, "The school district's policy clearly violates the free speech and free exercise rights of our client by denying her the ability to express her faith through the visible wearing of the necklace."[4] Once the lawsuit was filed, the school backed down and agreed to accommodate the religious beliefs of students.

Kandice Smith had to fight to keep her constitutional right to wear that cross around her neck. How many other students around the country have been told, "You can't wear that cross in school"? And how many children have simply tucked that dangerous cross inside their clothing or left it at home where it can't threaten anyone or create an offense?

How many times has the cross been taken away—and the rest of us never even heard about it?

When the Communists took the crosses away, they acted like thugs. They tore down the crosses and put red stars in their places. But in America, the government is more subtle when it removes the crosses from view.

The United States Capitol Visitor Center (CVC) was opened to the public on December 2, 2008, at a cost of $621 million ($200 million over budget). It was designed to serve as a gathering place, rest stop, and information center for the thousands of visitors who come to the United States Capitol complex every year.

When Senator Jim DeMint of South Carolina took a preview tour, he was dismayed to find that the CVC seemed to have scrubbed all references to God and America's religious heritage from its displays. There were references to Earth Day and casinos, but no references to churches and no images of steeples or crosses. A panel on one wall incorrectly stated that America's national motto is "E Pluribus Unum," meaning "Out of Many, One," when in fact our national motto was established by an act of Congress in 1956 as "In God We Trust."

One display features a replica of the Speaker's Rostrum in the House Chamber, yet omits the words "In God We Trust" inscribed in gold letters above the chair. Photos of the Speaker's Rostrum in the display have the words either cropped out or washed out so they are unreadable. The omission seems deliberate.

Another odd omission is found in a display of the Constitution. The "attestation clause" immediately before the Framer's signatures should read, "Done in Convention by the Unanimous Consent of the States present the Seventeenth Day of September in the Year of our Lord one thousand seven hundred and Eighty seven.... " But the CVC version omits the words "in the Year of our Lord."

One exhibit displayed the table upon which President Lincoln placed his Bible during the second inauguration—but just the table was there, no Bible. Senator DeMint was particularly troubled by an inscription at the entrance that read, "We have built no temple but the Capitol. We consult no common oracle but the Constitution."

These are just a few of the many instances in which it is clear that the designers of The Capitol Visitor Center took great pains to edit all references to God, faith, churches, and the cross out of its displays. Senator DeMint, Rick Tyler of Renewing American Leadership, Congressman Randy Forbes of Virginia, and others raised objections and offered suggestions for correcting these deficiencies and inaccuracies, and the CVC has fixed some of these

WHEN THE CROSSES ARE GONE

problems. But the fact remains that almost two-thirds of a billion dollars of taxpayer money was spent to present a distorted and godless image of America to Capitol visitors.[5]

This is just part of a deliberate effort to remove the cross—the *dangerous* cross—from American history and American life.

A Secular Taliban

In 1957, the Los Angeles County Board of Supervisors introduced a county seal that featured images representing the history, culture, and commerce of the county. The dominant image was that of Pomona, the Roman goddess of fruit trees, and it was surrounded by images of engineering instruments, a Spanish galleon representing early explorers, a fish, oil derricks, a dairy cow, the Hollywood Bowl, two stars representing the entertainment industry—and a small cross. The cross signified the influence of the early Spanish missions.

In 2004, the American Civil Liberties Union threatened to sue Los Angeles County if it did not remove the cross from the seal. According to the ACLU, the cross on the seal violated the "establishment clause" of the First Amendment, which says, "Congress shall make no law respecting an establishment of religion." This clause was intended to prevent America from establishing an official state church, such as the Church of England.

But does that tiny cross violate the establishment clause, as the ACLU claims? Of course not. It does not establish a "Church of Los Angeles County," nor does it show preference to the Christian religion over any other. That little cross simply acknowledges the fact that Catholic missions played a major role in the history of Los Angeles County. To erase that cross is to revise history.

As commentator Dennis Prager—who is Jewish—observed, "The cross represents the Christian history of Los Angeles County. It no more advocates Christianity than the Goddess Pomona advocates Roman paganism or the cow promotes Hinduism."[6]

The history of Los Angeles County is intertwined with the history of the early missions. The name "Los Angeles" ("The Angels") was given by Father Juan Crespi in 1769. It is a shortened form of "El Pueblo de Nuestra Señora la Reina de los Ángeles del Río de Porciúncula" ("The River of Our Lady the

6

Queen of the Angels of Porciuncula River (from the Spanish translation)").[7] So if the ACLU wants to erase the Christian history of Los Angeles County from its seal, we'll have to remove "Angeles" ("Angels") from the name. The same could be said for other American cities whose names reflect the influence of Christianity, such as Corpus Christi ("The Body of Christ") and Las Cruces ("The City of the Crosses").

When the ACLU threatened to sue, the Los Angeles County Board of Supervisors acted with all the courage and conviction we have come to expect from our elected officials: They caved in! They voted 3-2 to surrender to pressure from the extremist ACLU and remove the cross, replacing it with a picture of a crossless Spanish mission. When critics complained that the mission image looked like a "Taco Bell" fast-food restaurant, the supervisors replaced it with an image of Mission San Gabriel Arcángel—an image which some say makes the mission look like a barn.

The supervisors' decision was protested not only by Christians, but by Jews, Buddhists, and others who said that it is wrong to tamper with history. But the board feared the ACLU more than it feared its own citizens. The offensive cross had to be expunged. The American Civil Liberties Union (which is partly funded by our tax dollars!) is engaged in a relentless campaign to scrub every trace of Christian expression from our public life and our history.

Dennis Prager calls the ACLU "an American version of the Taliban." The Taliban, of course, is the Muslim extremist political movement who dynamited two sixth-century Buddha statues at Bamyan, Afghanistan, in 2001. The Taliban wanted to erase Afghanistan's non-Muslim history as if it had never happened— and the ACLU is engaging in the same kind of religious cleansing of America. "Giving in to the ACLU's threat is an act of cowardice," Prager writes, adding, "Los Angeles County is the largest county in America. If it allows its past to be expunged by a vote of three to two, America's past is sure to follow."[8]

Cowardice prevailed. The cross is gone. It was too dangerous, too offensive to depict on the county seal, even as an accurate and truthful symbol of the county's history.

The cross is treated as offensive not only in America, but in England and throughout Western civilization. In October 2006, British Airways told Nadia Eweida, a Christian employee, that she could not wear a cross necklace unless

7

she tucked it into her blouse where it could not be seen. Eweida had a seven-year unblemished record with the company, but when British Airways told her she could not wear a modest symbol of her religious faith, she refused to comply. She pointed out that British Airways allowed Sikh and Muslim employees to wear their religious symbols. Why could the Sikhs wear their iron bangles and turbans and the Muslims their hijabs, but the Christian cross was forbidden?

Eweida appealed her case to company arbitrators, but they denied her appeal. Only when British Prime Minister Tony Blair and the Archbishop of Canterbury raised a public protest did British Airways finally "just do the sensible thing" (as Blair put it) and permit Eweida to wear the cross.[9]

Why are the religious symbols of a Muslim or Sikh acceptable, while the cross of Christ is offensive... and even dangerous?

The Cross Conundrum

In November 2006, the College of William and Mary removed a cross from, of all places, the campus chapel. That's right, the *chapel*. In an email to the staff, the campus administrator wrote, "In order to make the Wren Chapel less of a faith-specific space, and to make it more welcoming to students, faculty, staff and visitors of all faiths, the cross has been removed from the altar area." The cross had been a part of Wren Chapel for more than 60 years.

Located in Williamsburg, Virginia, the College of William and Mary was established in 1693 as an educational institution of the Anglican Church, and is the second oldest institution of higher learning (after Harvard University) in the United States. The college became a non-denominational, publicly supported institution in 1906.[10]

The decision to remove the Wren Chapel cross ignited a storm of protest, but college president Gene Nichol explained the decision by saying that the cross would be offensive to non-Christian students. One alumnus of the college launched a website, SaveTheWrenCross.org, and quickly gathered thousands of names on its petition. Other alumni contacted the college, promising to withhold donations until the cross was restored to its rightful place.[11]

Finally, after nearly two months of heated controversy, Nichol made a minor concession, admitting that he "acted too quickly and should have consulted more broadly" before removing the cross. He ordered that the cross be placed on the altar—on Sundays only—and that a plaque be added to the chapel to commemorate its origins as "an Anglican place of worship and symbol of the Christian beginnings of the College." In short, Wren Chapel will be a true chapel with a Christian cross just one day a week; the rest of the week, the dangerous cross will be removed from the view.

President Nichol's "compromise" didn't satisfy those who wanted cross restored. "It is the Wren Chapel, not the Wren Spare Room," observed alumnus Karla Bruno. "If a visitor is insulted by the history and tradition of William and Mary and chooses... not to apply to the College for admission perhaps that is just as well. We should not be remodeling ourselves to suit a particular sort of applicant—the very narrow sort."

Nichol argues that the presence of the cross makes some feel "uncomfortable" (he claimed that twenty or so people had complained to him about the Wren Cross). Yet the *removal* of the cross offended *thousands* of people. Why do the feelings of twenty opponents of the cross outweigh the feelings of *thousands* who support the cross?

One student summed up the conundrum of the Wren Chapel cross this way: "In the name of tolerance, we have intolerance; in the name of welcoming, we have hostility, and in the name of unity, we now have division."[12]

Even within the institutional church, the cross has been called an offense. An interfaith group, the American Clergy Leadership Conference (ACLC), calls for churches to remove their crosses. Why? Because, according to this group, the cross is a symbol of oppression and represents an attitude of superiority. The elimination of the cross from Christian churches would help "tear down the walls that separate us as people of faith," says ACLC spokesman George Augustus Stallings, Jr., archbishop of the Imani Temple African American Catholic Church in Washington, D.C.

But doesn't the cross symbolize the love of God in offering us salvation through faith in Christ's death and resurrection? Stallings insists that the cross sends a message of hostility. "We have held up this cross in the face of Jews to say, 'If it had not been for your rejection of Jesus, our Messiah would never have been crucified,'" he said. "We also know that the cross has stood as a barrier in Christian-Muslim relationships because we have held up our cross as a superior faith, that we—as Christians—are superior over the Muslims."[13]

If any Christian has twisted the meaning of the cross as Stallings claims, then the fault is with that Christian, not with the cross. If any Christian has hated the Jews or treated Muslims with arrogance, then that Christian deserves blame—not the cross. The cross is a bridge which spans the gulf between God and humanity. The cross is not a wall of separation—it breaks down walls between people, bringing us all together as God's children. The message of the cross is a message of love.

That's the conundrum of the cross. In previous generations, the cross was an accepted symbol in our culture. A church steeple topped with a cross announced that *here* is a place where the message of God's love is preached. In our generation, however, the cross has become a dangerous thing—despised, hated, and rejected. We are just one generation away from seeing the departure of the Christian Gospel from our land.

Today, many evangelical churches, in an effort to be more "seeker-friendly" have decided not to identify their buildings with the symbol of the cross. Their intentions may be good. They certainly don't intend to compromise the Christian message. Within the building, they still proclaim the love of God through the cross of Christ. They simply don't want to place a symbol atop their building which might keep people away.

But though their intentions are good, they are taking a step toward compromise with the culture—a culture that is increasingly hostile toward the cross. By increments, they are departing from the truth. Without even realizing what they have done, these churches have elevated good public relations above a relationship with God. They have decided that it's more important to get people across the threshold and into the church than for the church to make a stand for the cross.

Whenever we elevate human wisdom above God's wisdom, we depart from *true* wisdom. The swaggering, self-sufficient spirit of humanity is expressed in the poem "Invictus," written in 1875 by William Ernest Henley. The poem contains these lines:

Out of the night that covers me,
Black as the pit from pole to pole,
I thank whatever gods may be
For my unconquerable soul....

It matters not how strait the gate,
How charged with punishments the scroll,
I am the master of my fate:
I am the captain of my soul.

To those who see themselves as the masters of their own fate, the captains of their own unconquerable souls, the wisdom of the cross is foolishness. The idea that God would come in human form and die upon a cross as a sacrifice for humanity, then rise from the dead to provide forgiveness of sin and eternal life—that is the height of foolishness! The very idea of the cross is so offensive that it must be eradicated from public view, from the public square, from churches and chapels, and even from the remotest reaches of the Mojave Desert.

The apostle Paul explained the cross conundrum this way: "For the message of the cross is foolishness to those who are perishing, but to us who are being saved it is the power of God" (1 Corinthians 1:18). In the original language, the Greek word for "message" was *logos* (λόγος), which contains several shades of meaning, including "word," "reasoning," or "logic." So it would be fair to translate Paul's statement, "For the logic of the cross is foolishness to those who are perishing." There is a logic to the cross which transcends human logic.

To those of us who have accepted the logic of the cross, there is no symbol in heaven or on earth more powerful, comforting, and inviting than the cross. As my friend the late John Stott, the Anglican clergyman and author, expressed it, "We are not allowed to envisage [God] on a deck-chair, but on a cross. The God who allows us to suffer once suffered himself in Christ, and continues to suffer with us and for us today.... I could never myself believe in God, if it were not for the cross. The only God I believe in is the One Nietzsche ridiculed as 'God on the cross.' In the real world of pain, how could one worship a God who is immune to it?"[14]

Only a superficial or hostile thinker could look at the cross and see a symbol of religious oppression or arrogance. The cross is a profound conundrum, a paradox, and the paradoxical logic of the cross tells us that hope springs from despair, life springs from death, and faith springs from our struggle with doubt and unbelief. The logic of the cross tells us that sinful human beings can be declared righteous in God's eyes—not because of anything they have done, but purely because God Himself died on a cross. This idea is absurd according to human logic; but that is the logic of the cross.

Let's be candid: The cross *is* dangerous. The cross *is* offensive. It is *meant* to disturb us. The message of the cross saws across the grain of the mood of our culture. It tells us, "You are *not* the master of your fate. You are *not* the captain of your soul. You are incapable of saving yourself. You are hopeless without a savior. In order for your life to have any meaning or hope, *someone else had to die.* Someone had to be tortured and killed in your place." That is an offensive message. That is the logic—and the offense—of the cross. Max Lucado offers an apt analogy:

> The cross is the universal symbol of Christianity. An odd choice, don't you think? Strange that a tool of torture would come to embody a movement of hope. The symbols of other faiths are more upbeat: the six-pointed star of David, the crescent moon of Islam, the lotus blossom for Buddhism. Yet a cross for Christianity? An instrument of execution?
>
> Would you wear a tiny electric chair around your neck? Suspend a gold-plated hangman's noose on the wall? Would you print a picture of a firing squad on a business card? Yet we do so with the cross. Many even make the sign of the cross as they pray. Would we make the sign of, say, a guillotine?[15]

The Latin word for cross is *crux*. It is fitting because the cross is literally the crux, the heart, of the Christian message. Remove the cross and you eliminate the essence of Christianity. So those who seek to remove the cross from our culture—whether it is the Soviet Communists or the ACLU or a college president or some misguided elements within the Christian Church—are perpetrating the worst form of religious intolerance. They are attacking the core truth of Christianity and seeking to eradicate it—because, to them, both Christianity and its cross are dangerous and offensive.

An Orderly, Rational Society

I am an American, but I was not born here. I came to America from Egypt and I became a naturalized American citizen. As a loyal adopted son of this great land who has accepted me, I fear for her future.

Those who would eradicate the cross from our land have also undermined the Constitution. They don't seem to understand that the First Amendment contains not one but *two* clauses regarding religion. The first is "the establishment clause"—which is the only clause the secularists seem to want to enforce. The second is "the free exercise clause." Together, these two clauses read: "Congress shall make no law respecting an establishment of religion, *or prohibiting the free exercise thereof.*" The second clause, which I have italicized, is generally ignored when the secular left talks about the First Amendment.

Watch news coverage of any First Amendment case and you will probably notice that the secularists, led by the ACLU, almost never quote the actual language of the First Amendment. Instead, they parrot the slogan "separation of church and state." Many Americans believe that the phrase "separation of church and state" comes from the U.S. Constitution—but there is no such language anywhere in the Constitution. (However, Article 124 of the 1947 constitution of the now-defunct Soviet Union *does* say that "the church in the USSR is separated from the state and the school from the church.")[16] If the words "separation of church and state" are not found in our Constitution, where do they come from?

In 1802, while President of the United States, Thomas Jefferson used that phrase in a letter to the Danbury Baptist Association of Connecticut. He wanted to assure the Danbury Baptists that the federal government would never infringe upon the free exercise of their religious faith. He wrote, "I contemplate with sovereign reverence that act of the whole American people which declared that their legislature should 'make no law respecting an establishment of religion, or prohibiting the free exercise thereof,' thus building a wall of separation between Church & State."[17]

The "wall of separation" Jefferson describes was designed to protect religion from government interference. Jefferson would be shocked and offended to know that the First Amendment is now being used by the ACLU and other secularists to *suppress* the free exercise of religion and to muzzle churches. When Jefferson wrote about "a wall of separation between Church & State," he never envisioned that his words would be twisted into a rationale for removing the cross from a schoolgirl's neck or from a war memorial or from a county seal.

If the American Civil Liberties Union is committed to defending our civil liberties, why doesn't it vigorously pursue violations of the free exercise clause? Why do the secularists seem so fanatically committed to removing all traces of God and faith from the public square? Does a memorial in the desert or a tiny cross on a child's necklace constitute the establishment of a state religion? Please! The very suggestion is an insult to reason.

The clear language of the First Amendment guarantees us the liberty to memorialize our war dead, to acknowledge the Christian history of our land, to recognize the Judeo-Christian influence on our founding documents, and to proclaim our national motto "In God We Trust." The First Amendment guarantees the right of a child to wear the cross in a public school, and guarantees our right to have America's religious heritage accurately represented at the Capitol Visitor's Center in Washington, D.C. The cross is an integral part of America's rich and diverse cultural heritage. But the secular forces in our society want to take those liberties away from us and our children.

When the crosses are gone, we will have lost everything: The protection of the Constitution. Our history. Our American heritage. Our liberty. And I think there is something else that is lost when the crosses are gone: We lose our ability to think clearly, to reason with one another, and to live together in an orderly, rational society.

Undermining Reason

The eradication of the cross from our national landscape is a symptom of our inability as a people to think rationally. Our Constitution is a rational document. The Bill of Rights is written in clear, straightforward English which is not difficult to understand. The letter President Thomas Jefferson wrote to the Danbury Baptists is equally clear and straightforward, and assures all people of faith that a wall of separation prevents the government from interfering with the free exercise of religion.

Today, however, the Constitution, the Bill of Rights, and Thomas Jefferson's statement of "separation between Church & State" have been turned upside down. Our government intrudes repeatedly on religious freedom, suppressing the right of religious people to express their religious convictions in the public arena. According to today's interpretation of so-called "separation of church and state," religion must stay in its place and keep its mouth shut. When religion speaks, it must speak softly, behind closed doors—never in public where others might hear and be offended.

A prime example took place in Indiana, when the Elkhart Parks and Recreation Board denied True Vine Tabernacle permission to hold summer evangelistic meetings in a public park that was notorious for drug activity. The church told the Parks Board it wanted to go door to door in the neighborhood and invite residents to a summer service in the park.

The board denied the request *specifically* because it disapproved of the church's religious activities. In other words, the board violated the free exercise clause of the First Amendment. Board member Bob Minichillo put it bluntly: "The pope could come here, and I would turn him down. When you start to evangelize, saving souls, et cetera, and it's done publicly—it's not going to happen in the park."[18]

This mindset says that religious "freedom" is only for private worship, behind closed doors. The free exercise of religion—such as evangelizing and saving souls—should not be practiced publicly.

But that's not religious freedom. Any "closet believer" in Communist China or the old Soviet Union or in the Islamic Republic of Iran can hide behind closed doors with a few other believers, reading the Bible and praying in whispers.

But the freedom to worship privately, behind closed doors, is not true First Amendment freedom.

The First Amendment clearly states, "Congress shall make no law respecting an establishment of religion, or prohibiting the free exercise thereof; or abridging the freedom of speech...." That means that Congress cannot prohibit the free exercise of religion and freedom of speech—including the freedom to evangelize and save souls in the park. If Congress cannot infringe on those rights, neither can the Elkhart Parks and Recreation Board.

Certainly, the board has the right to regulate certain activities within the park, such as skateboarding or dog-walking or littering. But it is plainly unconstitutional to prevent a church from evangelizing and saving souls and freely exercising its religion in the park. The board's actions reflect the anti-religious feeling of our times, but we are not to be governed by emotions. We are governed by a Constitution and by reason.

In December 2009, Secretary of State Hillary Clinton gave an address at Georgetown University's Gaston Hall, in which she said that people "must be free to choose laws and leaders; to share and access information, to speak, criticize, and debate. They must be free to worship, associate, and to love in the way that they choose."[19] In response, Christian commentator Charles Colson observed:

> In just two sentences, Mrs. Clinton revealed the government's desire to diminish freedom of religion and elevate the gay agenda to the level of an inalienable human right.... Twice in her speech, Mrs. Clinton referred to freedom of worship, but freedom of worship is not the same as freedom of religion, which is guaranteed in the Bill of Rights....
>
> The distinction between freedom of worship and freedom of religion is critical.... Freedom of religion is from God.... No secretary of state, no government has the right to take it or define it away.[20]

It's true. The opponents of religious liberty don't want us to think in terms of the actual wording of the First Amendment, which guarantees the free exercise of religion—*in the public square, not just behind closed doors.* They want us to think in terms of slogans like "separation of church and state" and "freedom of worship," because these slogans limit our ability to think clearly and rationally about our rights and religious liberties.

This is all part of a deliberate attempt to undermine rational thought in our culture. The ACLU would have us believe that a war memorial out in the middle of the desert is the equivalent of establishing the Church of England as a state religion. This is not rational, yet it is mainstream secularist thinking.

The secularists would have us believe that if one person is offended by a cross on a necklace or a county seal, then that cross must be removed. But if 100 million people are offended by the *removal* of that cross, well, that's just too bad. The many must bow to the whims of the few. The offended minority rules. This is not rational. In fact, it is madness. Yet it is mainstream thinking in our schools, our media, our government, and increasingly in our churches.

This book is a diagnosis of that madness—and a prescription for restoring sanity to a world gone mad. In the following chapters, we will examine several arenas in the life-and-death cultural struggle of feelings versus truth, including:

The Media: Our news outlets no longer make a pretense of objectivity. Instead, feelings-based indoctrination now permeates print and broadcast news. Front-page stories are routinely slanted to sway readers' emotions and manipulate their opinions. News has become propaganda.

The Government: Our political institutions routinely violate the clear intentions of the Founding Fathers, catering to the feelings-dominated mood of the moment. Politicians cynically deceive the voters with emotional appeals, promising the people whatever they want to hear— and knowing they will never be held accountable.

The Education Establishment: Our schools no longer teach young people how to think for themselves, how to reason, and how to recognize propaganda and logical fallacies. History is being rewritten so as not to hurt the feelings of this or that political pressure group. The Judeo-Christian foundation of our culture is under relentless attack.

The Family: Families are disintegrating throughout our nation and our Western culture. When I counsel troubled couples, I find the most common reason they give for dissolving their marriage is, "I just feel that the marriage is over." Warring emotions dominate—and often destroy—American families.

The Church: It may be a good marketing strategy for churches to appeal to the emotions. After all, superficial "feel-good" spirituality can fill the collection plate. But that's not God's strategy for advancing His kingdom and transforming lives.

In the final chapter, I will lay out a strategy for becoming agents of change and redemption in a world gone mad. I will show how you and I can become people of moral principles and objective faith, projecting truth and rationality to a world that has lost its mind.

When the crosses are gone, the world has truly gone mad. But we don't have to accept the madness. Just as a great fire can begin with a few sparks, great renewal can begin with a few committed individuals. Let's become agents of reason and truth in a world of lies. Let's become agents of sanity in a world gone mad.

Turn the page with me. Let's reason together, you and I.

Chapter Two

Feelings Versus Facts

On the night of July 16, 1999, thirty-eight-year-old John F. Kennedy, Jr., the son of the thirty-fifth president of the United States, piloted his single-engine Piper Saratoga from New Jersey to Martha's Vineyard, Massachusetts. With him were his wife, Carolyn, and sister-in-law, Lauren Bessette, and they planned to attend the wedding of a Kennedy cousin, Rory Elizabeth Kennedy.

Kennedy had logged 310 hours of flight time, though he had only completed half of an instrument training course. He'd made that trip many times at night. On this particular night, there was no moon, and a haze obscured the shore lights, making it hard to see the horizon.

The motion of the plane can fool the senses, especially at night. The aircraft's instruments, however, are objective. They show whether the plane is level, banking, climbing, or descending. If a pilot trusts his instruments, he can't go wrong. If he trusts his feelings, he risks what pilots call "the graveyard spiral."

That's what happened to John F. Kennedy, Jr.

When his plane was thirty miles from its destination, radar showed it right on course, heading for the airstrip. But at twenty miles out, Kennedy inexplicably made two turns *away* from the airstrip. Those turns sent the plane into an unrecoverable spiral, falling at 5,000 feet per minute. It crashed into the sea, sixteen miles from Martha's Vineyard. Kennedy and his passengers died instantly.

According to investigators, the crash was caused by a perception problem called "spatial disorientation." Flying in the dark, Kennedy lost his sense of direction and equilibrium. He either ignored or distrusted his instruments.

Kennedy's plane was equipped with an autopilot that could have taken over and returned the plane to straight and level flight—if he had simply switched it on. But he didn't. He relied on his subjective feelings and his feelings betrayed him.[1]

"Trust Your Feelings"

Since the Age of Reason in the seventeenth century, Western culture has been built on a foundation of reason and objective truth. In the 1960s, however, our culture underwent a radical transformation. The entire Baby Boom generation was profoundly affected by a new way of looking at reality—a focus on inner, subjective experience instead of objective truth. The crucial year was 1967.

Early that year, Dr. Timothy Leary toured the country, speaking at college campuses with a psychedelic light-and-sound presentation called "The Death of the Mind." He urged students to experiment with LSD, to start their own psychedelic religions, to turn off their rational minds and reach out to the universe with chemically altered feelings—to "turn on, tune in, and drop out."

The summer of 1967 was known as the "Summer of Love." Hundreds of thousands of hippies converged on cities across America, Canada, and Europe. The biggest gathering was in San Francisco, where 100,000 hippies descended on the Haight-Ashbury district. The "Summer of Love" was a massive culture-wide experiment with psychedelic drugs, acid rock music, promiscuous sex, and political rebellion. Years later, Time magazine said that the overriding theme of the "Summer of Love" was "trust your feelings."[2]

In August of that year, the Beatles had their first encounter with the Maharishi Mahesh Yogi. By the following year, the Beatles were promoting transcendental mysticism and Eastern religion to an entire generation.[3] Those three events in 1967—the college tours of Timothy Leary, the drug-drenched "Summer of Love," and the Beatles' promotion of Eastern spirituality—infected the Baby Boom generation with a deadly message: Turn off your mind. Trust your feelings.

Ten years later, that message was blasted into our collective consciousness with the release of George Lucas' *Star Wars* (1977). In the film, the wise mentor Obi-Wan Kenobi instructed young Luke Skywalker, "Trust your feelings!"

The Baby Boomers have turned gray. The "Summer of Love" hippies are living on Social Security. They have taught the "trust your feelings" worldview to their children and grandchildren, so that today's youth are even more divorced from rational thinking than their parents were. A feelings-based worldview pervades our culture.

We even see a "trust your feelings" mindset promoted by so-called "experts" on psychology and relationships. One bestseller, written by a noted psychiatrist and radio talk show host, tells us, "In feelings there is wisdom, for the simplest feelings speak the greatest truth.... Become comfortable with your feelings, because your feelings are your life.... Trust your feelings. They're the only true guidance you'll ever get."[4]

A current book for women, which the author calls "a simple guide to fun, sexy, happy, and easy relationships," contains a chapter called "Trust Your Feelings, Not Your Reasoning." There the author tells her readers, "So don't trust your thinking. It could be warped. Pay attention to your emotions, feelings, and moods, because they are clear indicators of the quality of your thinking, your current level of consciousness.... Emotions have their own logic. They are linked to an inner knowing that we can trust."[5]

This is an astounding statement: Thinking may be warped. Reason leads you astray. What makes you wise? Emotions, feelings, and moods! Is this true? Let's see where this advice leads us.

Suppose you see someone on a window ledge forty stories above the street, preparing to jump. This person is suicidal and may well be clinically depressed. The deadly emotions he or she feels at this moment could be due to some catastrophic life event, or emotions of guilt, or even an imbalance of neurotransmitter chemicals in the brain. What should we tell that person? "Trust your feelings! Your emotions speak the greatest truth!" What cruel and heartless advice! You might as well say, "Jump!"

Or consider this: Would you send your teenager out on a date saying, "Have a good time—oh, and whatever you do, don't trust your thinking! Trust your emotions!" A parent who gives such advice should be committed.

Suppose a driver cuts you off on the freeway—how should you respond? Well, you could trust your feelings. You could follow your emotions. Such a response is called "road rage."

Or suppose your spouse comes to you and confesses, "I've been having lustful feelings for someone at the office. I think I should quit my job and eliminate the temptation." What would you tell your spouse? "Oh, no, honey! Don't trust your thinking! It could be warped! Trust your emotions! Follow your feelings!" You would have to be insane or unloving to say such a thing.

Yet the advice to "trust your feelings" is called "wisdom" in our culture today.

"We All Buy on Emotion and Justify with Fact"

Our world has gone mad. We have discarded the rule of law and the rule of reason, and we have put feelings and emotions in their place.

We base government policy on the emotion of *pity*. We pity the poor, so we create the welfare state—and in the process, we reward dependency, irresponsibility, fraud, and victimhood. What we reward, we get more of—more poverty, more crime, more drug abuse, and more fatherless children. African-American news analyst Angela McGlowan describes the crisis we have inflicted on poor and minority families via the welfare state:

> In the late '50s and early '60s... liberal social planners were busy building the modern welfare state that would someday trap and destroy poor and minority families.... These policies pulled the rug of self-reliance out from underneath women and inner-city blacks and leave them trapped in a cycle of dependency....
> When black illegitimacy rates began soaring, with single black mothers increasingly becoming the rule rather than the exception, it was easier for liberals to advocate the expansion of the welfare state as a way to fill the gaps.... What government gives you, it can take from you. And what liberal welfare policies took from black Americans is beyond compare.[6]

We also base government policy on the emotion of envy. We envy the rich, so we tax them and punish them for being rich. We confiscate the earnings of small-business owners who produce the vast majority of jobs in our society, punishing industriousness, hard work, job creation, and achievement. Then we wonder why businesses are failing, unemployment is rising, and our economy is collapsing. It is because we base social policy on feelings and emotions instead of the Constitution, the moral law of God, and our God-given ability to think and reason.

The elimination of the crosses from our public square is a symptom of a deeper illness, a more fundamental madness that grips our society. It is the madness of allowing our society to be ruled by emotion rather than truth. This madness has infected our media, our government, the voting public, our schools, our families, and our churches. When the crosses are gone, it will be the result of our collective inability to reason on the basis of principles and moral laws.

This is not to say that emotion has no role to play in our society. It certainly does. In 1941, President Roosevelt appealed to our feelings of moral outrage after the attack on Pearl Harbor—and America responded, committing its forces to defeat the Axis powers in World War II. In 1962, President Kennedy appealed to our collective feelings of pride in achievement, calling for America to send astronauts to the Moon and return them safely to Earth—and America responded, achieving that goal in 1969. Churchill's "Blood, Toil, Tears and Sweat" speech, on his first day as Britain's new Prime Minister in 1940, inspired England to keep fighting against a seemingly invincible enemy. Entire nations can be moved to achieve lofty goals through the power of emotion.

But our emotions must be ruled by the law and governed by reason. Adolf Hitler used his powers of persuasion to incite emotions of fear and hatred against the Jews and other minorities, and to propel Nazi Germany into a war of conquest against its neighbors. With the passage of the Enabling Act of 1933, Hitler had the power to establish laws by his own decree. There was no Constitution to limit his power, so he was able to stir up the emotions of the nation with his words—then issue decrees to murder the Jewish people and plunge the world into war.

In America at the time of the Revolution, the Founding Fathers knew that no single leader could be trusted with the power of a dictator. They designed the Congress and the Supreme Court to be thoughtful, deliberative bodies that would slow the pace of decision-making, so the nation would never make a hasty decision in the emotion of the moment. As checks and balances on the power of the President, these co-equal branches of the government are intended to ensure that the nation will always be governed by law and reason—not hot-blooded emotion.

According to the United States Constitution, Article I, Section 8, Congress has the power to declare war. The President can't declare war. That power is reserved to Congress alone. If the President wants to take the nation to war, he must first ask Congress to make a declaration. The Founding Fathers knew that emotions often undermine reason and good judgment—and that a President might commit America to war in the heat of anger. So they gave that awesome power to the Congress—a cumbersome, deliberative body. The power to make war is divided among hundreds of members of Congress to ensure that reason and law, not emotion, govern our nation when the threat of war looms.

In recent years, politicians have become highly sophisticated at manipulating the emotions of voters. In speeches and campaign advertising, they cleverly use words and images which tap into our worst fears, our prejudices, our sense of outrage, our love for our children, and our hopes and dreams for the future. Instead of appealing to our reason, and telling us honestly what their political agenda truly is, they try to say as little as possible of substance, while ruthlessly manipulating our emotions.

Our feelings and emotions are more powerful than we realize. Communications expert Bert Decker puts it this way: "We all buy on emotion and justify with fact."[7] In other words, all of us as human beings tend to make emotion-based decisions; then, once the decision is made, we come up with a dozen fact-based reasons to justify that emotional decision. We fool ourselves into thinking that we have reached a reasonable conclusion. The truth is that our feelings and emotions were the decisive factor all along.

Decker suggests, for example, that we often choose to buy a certain house because it has charm or it is quaint or the paneling matches our furniture—

and we downplay all the facts that weigh against buying that house: it is in the wrong neighborhood, the plumbing leaks, the wiring is shot, and we can't afford the payments. So we buy on emotion—and only when it is too late do we realize that, in the light of logic and evidence, we have made a terrible decision.[8]

That, unfortunately, is also how we choose our national leaders, how we make fiscal and social policy, and on and on. Our leaders manipulate our emotions. We are led around like sheep because we have lost the ability to think clearly and to base our decisions on truth and timeless principles.

Mr. Decker's maxim, "We all buy on emotion and justify with fact," might well be the epitaph of Western civilization.

Setting the Thermostat

I once heard a story about a boy, the son of missionaries, who spent many of his early years in a boarding school. He was very young when he arrived at the school, alone and frightened. Because many of the students were separated from their parents for the first time in their lives, these children often cried themselves to sleep at night.

Years later, when the boy prepared to enter college, he met with a guidance counselor and described the emotional pain he suffered at boarding school. "One of the rules," he said, "was that we were only allowed to cry during our first three nights at the school. If a student cried after the third night, he was punished. I made sure I didn't get punished."

The counselor asked, "But what did you do with your tears if you couldn't cry out loud?"

"I cried in my stomach," the boy replied.

We can make all the rules we want, including a rule which says, "Don't cry or you'll be punished!" But we can't deny the reality of our emotions. They are an essential part of what makes us human. In fact, our emotions were given to us by God. Jesus sanctified human emotions by exemplifying them in His life. From the Scriptures, we know that Jesus laughed, became angry, and wept.

I do not disparage or devalue emotions. I am an emotional person myself. Emotions add excitement and sparkle to our lives, and our feelings truly make us human. It is no wonder that a person who never displays emotion is often described as a "robot."

Our warm, loving emotions keep us connected to the ones we care about most—friends and family, husband or wife, parents and children, and God. The Bible tell us that the greatest commandment is, "Love the Lord your God with all your heart and with all your soul and with all your strength and with all your mind" (Luke 10:27). We are to love God with our emotions, with our minds, and with every ounce of our strength.

It's no coincidence that the word "emotion" contains the word "motion," or that people say, "I was deeply moved" when they experience strong feelings. The English word "emotion" comes from the Latin *exmovere* (*ex* = out, *movere* = move or motion). So emotions literally *move* us and prompt us to action.

While feelings often move us to take positive action, our feelings can also prompt us to act foolishly. Anger can move us to speak out against injustice— but it can also move us to lash out in revenge or say things we later regret. How do we keep ourselves from making fools of ourselves in the heat of an emotional moment?

I recently visited my old friend, the late John R.W. Stott, Rector Emeritus of All Souls Church, Langham Place, and the author of such insightful books as *Basic Christianity* and *The Cross of Christ*. We talked about the danger of allowing ourselves to be controlled by our emotions, and he suggested a wonderful analogy. "The mind," he said, "should be the thermostat which sets the temperature for the emotions."

If we could keep the thermostat analogy in mind at all times, we would make better, wiser decisions—and we would save ourselves a lot of embarrassment and grief. Our God-given emotions serve an important function in our lives, but we must not be ruled by them. Rather we must allow our minds, as the thermostat, to govern the temperature of our feelings. Our emotions may prompt us to action, but we must always filter our actions through the grid of the mind. The thermostat of reason must set the temperature of the emotions.

Throughout the Scriptures, we are commanded to love—but our love is not to be a worldly love, based on feelings alone. Instead, our love is to be like the love of Jesus Christ, rooted in obedience and a commitment to seek the best for others, regardless of our feelings.

What about anger? It, too, must be regulated by the thermostat of the mind. Sometimes, it's *right* to be angry! It should make us angry when a child is abused or when powerful men oppress those who are defenseless. But Paul reminds us, "In your anger do not sin" (Ephesians 4:26). Never let anger fester into hate. Be angry with sin—but love the sinner. That is how the thermostat of the mind and of biblical principles regulates the temperature for our emotions.

"Under Control" Versus "Out of Control"

Let me suggest four reasons why we must place our mental thermostat in control of our feelings:

First, *feelings change.* Our moods rise and fall. Our emotions are affected by many factors that have nothing to do with wisdom, truth, and reality. Movies, TV shows, plays, and books can make us laugh—or cry. Music affects our moods, provoking feelings of wistfulness, melancholy, excitement, or joy. Many people experience depression in the wintertime because the reduced sunlight affects the level of a light-sensitive hormone, melatonin, in the brain (a condition called "seasonal affective disorder").

Events in our lives or in the news can make us happy—or plunge us into despair. After the terror attacks of September 11, 2001, all of America experienced a collective mood of depression mingled with outrage.

Feelings are variable, like the weather. So we have to learn to set the thermostat of our emotions with our minds, in reliance on firm, unchanging principles.

Second, *feelings can be deceptive.* Our emotions reflect our inner state, not the objective reality of our lives. You can have a great job, a loving family, and money in the bank. But if you have a mood disorder (such as manic depression), your inner emotional state may be the exact opposite of your outward situation.

Sexual or romantic attraction is one of the most deceptive feelings of all. A young lady becomes infatuated with a young man. She looks at him through eyes of love and sees Prince Charming. Her friends look at him more objectively—and they see a Casanova, a playboy. They try to warn her—but she doesn't hear a word they say. If she follows her feelings alone, she may well be deceived—and she won't discover the truth until her heart is broken. Here again, the mind must be the thermostat which keeps emotions in check.

Third, *feelings do not consider consequences*. Over the years, I have counseled literally hundreds of people who have suffered broken marriages, the loss of families, unwanted pregnancies, or sexually transmitted diseases—because they relied on their feelings to make crucial moral decisions. They got swept up by passion or selfish desire, they refused to think about the consequences—but now they are *suffering* the consequences. The thermostat of the mind, rooted in sound, godly principles, would have prevented these tragedies.

Fourth, *feelings possess no wisdom*. Emotions do not help us analyze a situation in light of values, principles, or biblical truth. Moods do not give us a firm foundation for decision-making. Wisdom comes from thinking the right thoughts, heeding the right advice, learning the right lessons, and making the right choices.

So these are four reasons why we should not allow our feelings to set the "room temperature" for our decisions: Feelings often change. Feelings can deceive us. Feelings do not consider consequences and feelings do not make us wise.

The better we understand how our feelings affect our behavior and decision-making, the more effectively we can keep our emotions *under* thermostatic control—and the less likely we are to allow our words and behavior to get *out of* control. Unfortunately, our world functions as if its thermostat has gone haywire.

Easy Prey

In an address at the United Nation's Prayer Breakfast on October 30, 2007, Christian author Ravi Zacharias said, "We have lost our ability to reason.... Very few are able to think clearly anymore. I have often said the challenge of the truth speaker today is this: How do you reach a generation that listens with its eyes and thinks with its feelings?"[9]

Zacharias has described one of the greatest challenges Western civilization has ever faced. The Eastern world is largely governed by dictators and strongmen, but Western civilization is largely democratic. "We the People" choose our own leaders. Herein lies a great danger: If we are easily manipulated by emotional arguments, then we risk being misled, fleeced, and even conquered by political con men who know how to manipulate our emotions. We could easily hand our civilization over to a leader who is captivating, and beguiling—a leader with the voice of an angel, the charm of the movie star, and the heart of a devil.

As a democratic society, we desperately need to develop clear, well-reasoned viewpoints, based on facts, principles, and evidence. We must learn to evaluate the views and arguments of our leaders in a thoughtful and intelligent way. It is *literally* a matter of life and death.

In the 1970s, hundreds of people were seduced into a religious cult by a preacher named Jim Jones. His personal charisma and emotional style of preaching could charm the birds out of the trees. He founded his cult, The Peoples Temple, in Northern California, and eventually led his followers to Jonestown, a prison-like compound in Guyana.

When an American congressman flew to Guyana to inspect the compound, Jim Jones' henchmen murdered the congressman. Then Jones ordered his followers to commit "revolutionary suicide" by drinking cyanide—and 918 people lost their lives. Most died because they were swept away by the emotionally charged preaching of a manipulative con-man.

Every day, all over the world, well-meaning people are cheated out of their money, their health, their vote, their faith, or even their lives. Why? Because they are unable to rationally weigh the claims of swindlers, medical quacks, political demagogues, or religious hucksters. They are easy prey for any charlatan who can sway their emotions.

If we don't want to be cheated or controlled by others, we must learn to think skeptically, and to examine the evidence. We must learn to recognize— and not be taken in by—emotional appeals.

What is true for individuals is even truer for our entire society. We live in a dangerous world, surrounded by enemies who hate us and wish to destroy us and our way of life. Some of our enemies are nuclear-armed nations. Others are terrorists eager to obtain weapons of mass destruction and use them against us. If terrorists get their wish, the next attack may make the horrors of 9/11 pale in comparison. So all people, throughout Western society, need to make wise, rational, informed choices about the direction our civilization is going.

Living in the Land of "Whatever"

We live in a world where people get their "truth" from Oprah, or *The National Enquirer*, or the far fringes of the Internet. All around us are people who believe that George Bush and Dick Cheney blew up the World Trade Center, or that Elvis lives, or that actress Shirley MacLaine receives messages from her pet dog. Some people claim to have seen statues weep. Others say they have been abducted by space aliens in UFOs.

Perhaps one reason so many people give credence to such outlandish claims is that they have adopted the prevailing cultural mindset—a mindset which says that *objective truth doesn't matter*. If facts get in the way of your feelings-based worldview, then simply rearrange reality to your liking. Truth is whatever you want it to be. It's *your* truth, and no one has a right to question it.

There's a name for this mindset. It's called *postmodernism*.

As the name suggests, postmodernism is the worldview that is quickly replacing modernism. The old modernist worldview regarded reason, logic, and objective evidence as the pathway to truth. Modernists believed that the nature of the reality could be discovered by the scientific method.

Postmodernists reject the idea of objective truth. They say, "What is true for you is not necessarily true for me." They see all choices and opinions as equally valid. They believe feelings are just as reliable an ethical guide as reason. In fact, as social critic Robert Lightner explains, "Postmodernists believe that reason itself is a cultural bias of the modernistic, white, European male. If reason does not exist, truth is relative and all choices are equally valid. If all choices are valid, authority should be wholly rejected.... Therefore, postmodernism is inherently unstable. It breeds contradictions."[10]

Demographic researcher George Barna, founder of The Barna Group of Ventura, California, has conducted nationwide surveys which show that the postmodern worldview has infiltrated the Christian community. More than two-thirds of Christians who call themselves "born-again" have a worldview that is distinctly postmodern as opposed to the biblically Christian. Vast numbers of Christians now find abortion, drunkenness, pornography, cohabitation, and homosexual behavior morally acceptable, in stark contrast to the teaching of Scripture. Barna concludes:

Without some firm and compelling basis for suggesting that such acts are inappropriate, people are left with philosophies such as "if it feels good, do it," "everyone else is doing it" or "as long as it doesn't hurt anyone else, it's permissible." In fact, the alarmingly fast decline of moral foundations among our young people has culminated in a one-word worldview: "whatever." The result is a mentality that esteems pluralism, relativism, tolerance, and diversity without critical reflection of the implications of particular views and actions.[11]

Barna tells us that the word "whatever" defines the mood of a generation. If you try to reason with some young people today, they will not argue with you. They will not support their opinions with facts. They will simply shrug and say, "Whatever." With that single word, they can dismiss all your logically consistent arguments. They can write off all your evidence and moral principles. "Whatever" means, "I reject your authority. I don't care what you say. Don't bother me."

In his 2007 address at the United Nation's Prayer Breakfast, Ravi Zacharias told of being invited to lecture at Ohio State University. As his host drove him to the lecture hall, they passed a campus building with a startling architectural design. Zacharias's host said, "That's the Wexner Center for the Performing Arts. It's America's first postmodern building."

Ravi Zacharias had heard of postmodern plays, films, books, and music, but not postmodern architecture. "What," he asked, "is a postmodern building?"

"Well," the other man replied, "the architect said he designed this building with no design in mind. When asked, 'Why?' he said, 'If life itself is capricious, why should our buildings have any design and any meaning?' So he has pillars that have no purpose and stairways that lead nowhere."

Zacharias said, "So he argues that if life has no design, why should the building have any design?... Did he do the same with the foundation?"

The man had no answer for that question.

Ravi Zacharias concluded, "You and I can fool with the infrastructure as much as we would like, but we dare not fool with the foundation because it will call our bluff in a hurry."[12]

Yet that is precisely what we have done in our culture. We have demolished the foundation of our society. Then we look around and wonder why everything is crumbling around our ears.

We are living in the land of "Whatever," and you cannot build a stable life or a sturdy culture on a foundation of "Whatever." The postmodern view of reality leads to despair.

A Debased View of the Constitution

As an old-fashioned immigrant, I cherish the godly heritage of America. I left Egypt, the land of my birth, and came to America because I deeply love the principles this nation was founded on. I especially love the principles embodied in the founding documents, The Declaration of Independence and the Constitution. I am amazed that so many people born on American soil have such a low regard for those principles.

A few years ago, a presidential candidate called the U.S. Constitution "a living and breathing document" that "was intended by our founders to be interpreted in the light of the constantly evolving experience of the American people."[13] In other words, as the public changes its mind (or its feelings), we should alter our interpretation of the Constitution.

In reply to this "living document" theory of constitutional interpretation, Supreme Court Justice Antonin Scalia said, "You would have to be an idiot to believe that. The Constitution is not a living organism, it is a legal document. It says some things and doesn't say other things."[14]

I can understand why some people want to stretch and twist the Constitution to mean whatever they want. If you operate on the basis of feelings instead of values and principles, the Constitution can be a very annoying document. If you feel you should have the right to abort unborn babies, and you can't find that right spelled out in the Constitution, then you need some imaginative judges to find it there like a fortune-teller reading tea leaves—which is precisely what five out of nine Supreme Court justices did in the 1973 Roe vs. Wade decision.

This adopted son of America thinks that the Constitution is just fine as it was written. If it needs to be changed, let's change it the way the Constitution says it should be changed—by an amendment process involving We the People, not by five over-reaching social engineers in black robes. I only have one vote to cast, but I vote that we restore the original intentions of the U.S. Constitution.

The people who founded this country put their lives on the line in order to preserve certain principles—sacred principles of freedom and equality. Thousands of patriots died laying the foundation of America. The mortar of that foundation was drenched with their blood—but they built a nation that has stood as a lighthouse of hope and freedom for more than two centuries.

As a young man, I stood on the far side of the world and saw the light of freedom shining from that lighthouse. It was the light of freedom that drew me here—but today that light is fading and one of the symptoms of the gradual loss of freedom in America is that the crosses are being removed from buildings and even from the necks of our children. So I am writing this book to sound the alarm—to plead with you, with all Americans, to listen and act before it is too late, before the light of freedom has gone out, before the crosses are all gone.

As an immigrant from the Middle East, I remember clearly what America used to be—and I see clearly what America is becoming. The change has been gradual—so gradual that those who were born here may not have even noticed. But I am a student of culture. Though I am fully American, I have traveled the globe and have lived my life with one foot in the West and one in the East. I am aware of the rapidly changing Western mindset. The transformation I am witnessing is nothing less than frightening. As I survey the American landscape, I see a culture that has not only lost its way, but is losing its mind.

We have replaced thinking with emotion. Our society makes crucial life-and-death decisions based purely on emotions. We disregard principles, evidence, objective truth, laws, moral standards, the plain sense of our Constitution, and the clear truth of God's Word. In their place we enshrine our subjective moods and feelings.

We remove the Christian cross from a war memorial in the desert, and from a county seal, and even from the altar of a Christian chapel—*not* because the First Amendment requires us to, but because we are afraid that the "dangerous" and "offensive" cross will hurt someone's feelings. In our unreasoning rush to remove the symbols that might offend the feelings of a tiny minority, we take away the constitutional rights of the majority. We offend the sensibilities of the majority. The removal of the crosses from our society is irrational and unconstitutional and wrong—yet it is happening all around us, everyday, and it will be our undoing.

On the night of July 16, 1999, young John F. Kennedy, Jr., flew his airplane into the sea, killing himself and his two passengers because he relied on his feelings instead of the objective evidence of his instruments. Today, our entire culture is flying through the darkness, ignoring the instruments of reason and truth, disregarding the principles of God's Word. And we, too, are headed for a crash.

Chapter Three

Restoring Sanity to the Media

Which is more offensive—the pop star Madonna impersonating the crucified Christ, or talking vegetables who say, "God loves you?"

In 2006, the NBC television network began airing the popular *Veggie Tales* series on Saturday mornings. The series, which featured the comic adventures of talking vegetables, had developed a huge and devoted following through sales of videotapes and DVDs. The stories featured positive values, and were often based on stories from the Bible. But when the series aired on NBC, network censors edited out references to God, including the familiar signoff message, "Remember, kids, God made you special and He loves you very much."

When young fans and parents demanded to know why the faith content had been cut out of the show, NBC replied that *Veggie Tales* had to be altered in order to meet "network broadcast standards." One NBC spokesperson said, "Our goal is to reach as broad an audience as possible with these positive messages while being careful not to advocate any one religious point of view."

Yet it's hard to understand how the message "God made you special and He loves you very much" can be considered exclusive to one religion. That message is consistent with the views of every Protestant denomination, the Roman Catholic Church, Judaism, Mormonism—in short, with the views of probably 95 percent of NBC's audience.

When parents object to violence or pornographic content on television, the networks' standard reply is, "If you don't like what we broadcast, just change the channel." But, as Brent Bozell of the Media Research Center points out, "When it comes to religious programming—programming that doesn't even mention Jesus Christ—just watch the hypocrisy. Instead of telling viewers to just change the channel if they don't like it... religion has to be shredded before broadcast."[1]

In fact, the same year the *Veggie Tales* controversy erupted, NBC aired a concert by pop singer Madonna. The concert had already made news because of Madonna's controversial performance of the song "Live to Tell," in which she rises up out of the stage fastened to a cross of mirrors, crucified with a crown of thorns on her head. When the network announced it would air the entire concert, including "Live to Tell," letters of protest flooded the NBC offices.

The network stood its ground, refusing to consider the objections of people of faith. It aired the Madonna concert with its sacrilegious imagery intact. Mentioning the love of God might be offensive to some, so it must be censored. Yet the blasphemous abuse of the Christian cross is perfectly acceptable to NBC, despite a huge public outcry. This is media hypocrisy at its worst.[2]

To demonstrate hypocrisy is to falsely claim to live by a set of consistent standards and beliefs. Hypocrisy often involves self-deception as well as the deceiving of others. It may well be that an agnostic or atheistic mindset on the part of some network executives prevents them from seeing the contradiction between the censorship of *Veggie Tales* and the airing of Madonna's offense (and even blasphemous) performance.

"It Is All Spin"

Media hypocrisy is just as prevalent in the news media as it is in the entertainment media. In mid-2007, *The New Republic*, an American magazine devoted to politics and the arts, published a series of articles by an American soldier identified as "Scott Thomas." The articles claimed to reveal, in shocking detail, how "Scott Thomas" and his fellow soldiers had committed despicable acts while on duty in Iraq.

The author claimed that he and other soldiers sat in an Army chow hall in Baghdad when a woman came in who had been gruesomely disfigured by an IED (improvised explosive device). He claimed that he ridiculed the woman, loudly calling her "crypt keeper" because she looked like a creature from a horror film. "The disfigured woman slammed her cup down," he wrote, "and ran out of the chow hall."

He also claimed that soldiers uncovered a mass grave filled with the skeletal remains of children, and that one Army private "marched around with [a piece of a child's] skull on his head." He described how a fellow soldier took joy rides in a Bradley Fighting Vehicle because "it gave him the opportunity to run things over. He took out curbs, concrete barriers, corners of buildings, stands in the market, and his favorite target: dogs." One dog, he said, "walked close enough for him to jerk the machine hard to the right and snag its leg under the tracks."

If those claims were true, "Scott Thomas" and his fellow soldiers had repeatedly violated the military code of justice. Why would a soldier admit such acts? A number of journalists questioned the truthfulness of the articles. In response, *The New Republic* identified the author: Army Private Scott Thomas Beauchamp, age twenty-three, stationed in Iraq. Beauchamp insisted his accounts were true.

The Army investigated and then announced that Beauchamp had recanted his claims under oath. But Beauchamp told his editors he had never recanted— he stood by the articles. *The New Republic* continued to back Beauchamp's tales, even as they began to crumble. When investigators couldn't find the disfigured woman in Baghdad, Beauchamp claimed the incident took place in Kuwait. When no such woman was found in Kuwait, the *New Republic* editors had to retract the story.

William Kristol, editor of *The Weekly Standard*, offered this explanation: "The editors [at *The New Republic*] must have wanted to suspend their disbelief in tales of gross misconduct by American troops. How else could they have published such a farrago of dubious tales?"[3]

In other words, the editors desperately wanted those stories to be true. They wanted to show the world that the Iraq War was turning our troops into soulless monsters who would taunt a burn victim, desecrate the remains of dead children, and run down dogs in the street. The editors' feelings overruled their judgment—and our military was falsely vilified.

We saw this same emotion-based bias at work in mid-2007, when the "surge strategy" in the Iraq War showed signs of success. The war-weary American people welcomed the good news that we had turned a corner in the Iraq War. But news of American success in Iraq didn't fit the "failed war" storyline that the news industry was pushing, so one news organization found a way to portray success as failure.

A McClatchy news story headlined "Iraqi Cemetery's Business Falls" told about Iraq's Wadi al Salam cemetery in Najaf. There, cemetery workers were forced to take pay cuts because of declining numbers of war dead to bury. Nowhere does the article mention the success of the surge strategy. Rather, the authors report on the dramatic decline of war deaths as if it were an accident of nature rather than an American success story:

> At what's believed to be the world's largest cemetery, where Shiite Muslims aspire to be buried and millions already have been, business isn't good. A drop in violence around Iraq has cut burials in the huge Wadi al-Salam cemetery here by at least one-third in the past six months, and that's cut the pay of thousands of workers who make their living digging graves, washing corpses or selling burial shrouds.[4]

Isn't that amazing? These reporters found a way to turn good news into tragedy! Think of all the good news that *could* have been reported—fewer military and civilian casualties, children who could safely play soccer in the streets, growing cooperation between Shiites and Sunnis, the defeat of Al Qaeda in Iraq. Yet these reporters could only find bad news: the "tragic" plight of Iraqi gravediggers.

We hear a lot today about "liberal bias" in the news but I believe there is an even more dangerous form of bias in the media today: *emotional bias*. No longer are reporters content to simply report events as they happen. Instead, they must give us an emotion-drenched drama, complete with heroes and villains. Emotionally biased reporting goes hand-in-glove with politically biased reporting. If you, as a reporter, lean toward a political viewpoint, then it's perfectly natural for you to portray those you agree with as heroes and those you don't as villains.

We live in a postmodern world in which journalists value "spin" over facts. They see objective truth as an illusion, and think feelings are as valid as facts. Just ask Mitchell Stephens, professor of journalism at New York University. In his article "We're All Postmodern Now" (*Columbia Journalism Review*, July/August 2005), he celebrates the new journalistic reality. The old objectivity-oriented reporters (Stephens calls them "fact-worshipping journalists") have given way to a whole new generation of reporters who "see through the pretense that news merely consists of collections of unbiased information." He explains:

> Facts often—on a grassy knoll in Dallas, for example—prove impossible to pin down. They often prove—as in Vietnam—malleable. And they often attach themselves—in Nicaragua, on the West Bank—to someone's perspective of an event.... In an age when information travels fast and arrives from numerous directions, collections of shiny little fact nuggets have become harder to sell.... The old twentieth-century line between fact and interpretation has become more difficult to draw (or pretend to draw).[5]

Stephens tells us that postmodern journalism is here to stay—and he says that is a *good* thing. Facts are troublesome and hard to sell—so journalists need to sell spin, opinion, and personal bias instead. In a postmodern world, news consumers no longer need to know who, what, where, when, and why. As Stephens concludes, "It's all spin."[6]

Today's postmodern journalist does not recognize the old objective standards of truth, journalistic excellence, or journalistic integrity. The result, increasingly, is journalistic chaos. Some examples:

AP Washington bureau reporter Christopher Newton was fired in 2002 for padding his stories with quotes from nonexistent people. *New York Times* reporter Jayson Blair, *USA Today* foreign correspondent Jack Kelly, Pulitzer Prize-winning *Sacramento Bee* columnist Diana Griego Erwin, *Boston Globe* freelance reporter Barbara Stewart, *Bakersfield Californian* health reporter

Nada Behziz, and *Richmond Times-Dispatch* political reporter Paul Bradley were all disgraced for publishing fabricated stories.[5] In 2004, *The Boston Globe* published photos that allegedly showed American troops raping Iraqi women; the photos turned out to be commercial pornography. A 2006 *U.S. News and World Report* cover photo, which supposedly showed a Hezbollah fighter at the site of an Israeli air strike, was actually taken at a burning tire dump.[7]

Many of these cases can undoubtedly be traced to postmodernism. When standards of truth and morality have been swept away, we open the door to journalistic malpractice.

Trapped by Our Templates

Bernard Goldberg spent nearly three decades as a CBS News correspondent. In *Bias: A CBS Insider Exposes How the Media Distort the News*, Goldberg wrote about the slanted reporting he had witnessed in his career. He also cited a survey of journalists conducted after the 1992 election. The survey found that 89 percent of journalists voted for Bill Clinton for president. This is more than double the 43 percent of non-journalists who voted for Clinton. "This is incredible when you think about it," Goldberg reflects. "There's hardly a candidate in the entire United States of America who carries his or her district with 89 percent of the vote. This is way beyond mere landslide numbers."[8]

If all reporters and editors see the world through the same mental filter, if they all share the same values and worldview, they will produce a homogenized news product. They will all tend to play down certain events, play up others, and present their subjective opinion as objective truth. This is because they view reality through a mental filter called a "template."

Amanda Bennett, a Pulitzer prize-winning reporter and now executive editor at Bloomberg News, coined the term "template" and defined it as "what editors... have decided is The Story." She developed this theory while reporting from Communist China in the 1980s. When she first began filing stories from that country, her editors "only wanted good stories about happy little children, beaming peasants, friendly people." The storyline they wanted was about how a progressive post-Mao China was improving the lives of its people. If Bennett filed a story about Chinese citizens being mistreated by their totalitarian government, the stories didn't get published. Only positive stories fit the editors' template.

Then came the Tiananmen Square uprising of 1989. Government suppression of the protests left hundreds dead—possibly as many as 3,000. Instantly, the template changed. "Now it was impossible to get a story in that said anything *good* about China," Bennett recalled. "All anyone wanted to hear about was human rights abuses."[9]

The template continues to warp journalistic judgment today. If a reporter submits a story that doesn't fit the template, the story may be killed; that's suppression of the truth. Or the editor may tinker with the story until it fits the template; that is distortion of the truth. Or the editor may accept a false story without checking simply because it fits the template so perfectly.

Whether we come from the left, right, or center of the spectrum, we all have our mental templates. It is human nature to screen out information that does not square with our assumptions. Like the prejudiced Pharisees whom Jesus spoke of, we all tend to "strain out a gnat but swallow a camel" (see Matthew 23:24).

The more we become aware of our templates, the more clearly, accurately, and objectively we can see reality. The moment we admit to ourselves that we "see through a glass darkly," we begin to question our assumptions. It is a matter of humility, an admission that we don't have all the answers. If a mental template can deceive some of the world's leading journalists, it can deceive us. A little humility will vaccinate us against pride and self-deception—and prevent us from becoming trapped by our templates.

Is bias in the media simply the result of a "herd mentality" in the news business—or is bias a deliberate conspiracy among journalists? Bernard Goldberg replies, "No conspiracies. No deliberate attempts to slant the news. It just happens.... News, after all, isn't just a collection of facts. It's also how reporters and editors see those facts, how they interpret them, and most important, what facts they think are newsworthy to begin with."[10]

On the whole, Goldberg is probably right. More recently, however, evidence of a deliberate media conspiracy has surfaced. In July 2010, a political website, *The Daily Caller*, published emails that were exchanged among several hundred prominent journalists and academics who were part of a left-leaning online group called JournoList. According to *The Daily Caller*, JournoList members included some of the elite commentators and reporters from such news organizations as "*Time*, Politico, the Huffington Post, the *Baltimore Sun*, the *Guardian*, Salon and the *New Republic*."

JournoList members huddled online to discuss ways to influence news coverage and even affect the kinds of questions to be asked in the presidential debates. One JournoList member urged fellow journalists to go on the attack against the conservative media, to (metaphorically) smash their conservative opponents "through a plate-glass window," then take "a snapshot of the bleeding mess and send it out in a Christmas card to let the right know that it needs to live in a state of constant fear.... Take one of them—Fred Barnes, Karl Rove, who cares—and call them racists."

After Republican candidate John McCain chose Alaska governor Sarah Palin as his running mate, JournoListers buzzed about a coordinated effort to destroy her politically. As members of the group bounced ideas back and forth, one JournoLister asked the group for talking points, saying, "Keep the ideas coming! who have to go on TV to talk about this in a few min and need all the help I can get."[11]

The emotionally charged, highly biased views that were exchanged on JournoList are exemplified by a public radio producer who described what she would do if she saw a certain conservative talk show host suffering a heart attack. Not only would she *not* call 911 for help, but she would actually "laugh loudly like a maniac and watch his eyes bug out" as he died. She added, "I never knew I had this much hate in me. But he deserves it." After her comments were revealed in *The Daily Caller*, she issued a public apology.[12]

Political science professor Jim Campbell of State University of New York finds the actions of JournoList troubling. "At one level it could be thought of as just colleagues throwing ideas out to one another," he said, "but from another standpoint it almost looks like collusion... where virtual talking points are shared and solidified in a group.... That can't be healthy for the country—or for the media."[13]

After *The Daily Caller* revealed the existence of JournoList, the online group disbanded. The demise of JournoList prompted Andrew Sullivan of *The Atlantic* to respond, "I'm glad Journo-list is over. It should never have been begun. I know many of its members are good and decent and fair-minded writers. But socialized groupthink is not the answer to what's wrong with the media. It's what's already wrong with the media."[14]

JournoList is no more. But media bias and media groupthink go on.

Eye-candy—Or Eye-poison?

Television is an emotionally powerful medium. It brings people and events close to us. The visual nature of television also makes that medium ripe for emotional manipulation—and sexual exploitation. And I'm not talking about shows like *Desperate Housewives* and *Grey's Anatomy*. I'm talking about the *news*.

Viewers were delighted when the Fox News Channel arrived on the scene in October 1996, promising "fair and balanced" reporting. News viewers, sick of mainstream media bias, fled to Fox News like refugees, quickly making it the number one cable news channel.

Alas, it was not long before Fox News began spicing up its "fair and balanced" coverage with segments about Victoria's Secret models or *Playboy* photo shoots—with plenty of sleazy footage. At times, Fox News has under-reported significant news events to join the celebrity news frenzy. While some Fox News shows have maintained a serious perspective, others frequently sink to the level of tabloid journalism. The news business must pay attention to ratings, but it should also take responsibility for its corrosive influence on our culture. As media consumers, we should demand accountability.

In her book *Power to the People*, radio commentator Laura Ingraham laments "the creeping tabloidization of cable news." Because she appears as a Fox News commentator, she's had many conversations with news producers about the sleazy topics and images the cable news networks exploit. TV producers reply that they "are only giving the people what they want" or "it gets huge ratings." Ingraham says that's faulty reasoning:

Did the viewers of MSNBC, Fox News Channel, and CNN band together to implore news directors that they wanted nonstop Anna Nicole Smith coverage?... Was America really demanding hundreds of hours of programming devoted to the Paris Hilton incarceration, the Scott Peterson murders, and the Mary Kay Letourneau teacher-student sex case?

This is not giving people what they want or need, it's giving people what they'll take. It's giving them what's easy—easy to produce, easy to market, easy to cover. Friends tell me that they find themselves getting "sucked into" these stories—it almost becomes a "tragedy TV" addiction. You get a little taste and you keep going back for more because it requires little critical thinking.[15]

It's sad, but true: the cable and network news media will continue to dumb down important issues and exploit sleaze for ratings. While the networks manipulate the emotions and lusts of the audience, thinking gets lost. We neglect the critical issues affecting our lives and our children's future. What seems like candy to the eyes is often poison to the soul and we sit in front of our flat-screen, high-definition, 500-channel TVs and consume that poisonous brew day after day, heedless of the consequences.

The Christian church used to take a stand against immorality on television. Today, broadcast and cable shows feature every lurid and degrading practice, from pornography to violent blood sports—and there's not a whimper of protest from the Christian community. We have allowed the secular media to intimidate us into silence. The dominant media has reframed the debate, portraying any voice of moral protest as the whining of a narrow-minded bigot. No one wants to be called a bigot—so Christians have muted their protest.

Meanwhile, the militant Islamic world rejoices that Western culture is on a downhill slide to destruction. The forces of extremism are already celebrating the death of our civilization. We in the West do not understand the threat we face. Since 9/11, Western political and social commentators have repeatedly said that the Islamic terrorists "hate our way of life." In other words, they attacked America because of America's sexual and permissive freedoms.

While that's true, Westerners don't seem to understand that it goes much further than that. Islamic extremists also hate the Christian ("Crusader") faith. They hate Western support for Israel. They hate our constitutionally-guaranteed freedom of speech, freedom of the press, and freedom of religion. Islamic fundamentalists seek to impose Shari'a law on the entire world (which would mean, among other things, the oppression of women everywhere). All human liberties would be suspended in favor of total submission to the Caliphate (Allah's ruler on earth). These are the important issues that the Western media, out of a misplaced devotion to "political correctness," fails to disclose to its viewers.

("Political correctness" is a mindset in which a person seeks to use words which avoid offending certain groups of people—especially racial groups, cultural groups, disability groups, and gender or sexual orientation groups. In principle, of course, it's laudable to want to be sensitive to the feelings of others. Unfortunately, the politically correct mindset is usually concerned primarily with the feelings of certain minority groups, including Muslim extremists, but generally does not hesitate to disparage America or offend Christians.)

I was saddened, a few years ago, to hear of the death of Russian author Aleksandr Solzhenitsyn. I had the pleasure of meeting this inspiring man when he received the Templeton Prize in 1983. Through his writings, he alerted the world to the horrors of the Soviet gulags. A dedicated Marxist-Leninist in his youth, Solzhenitsyn served as an artillery captain on the Eastern Front in World War II. During the war, he wrote a letter to a friend which included a mild criticism of the Soviet leader, Stalin. The letter was intercepted—and that comment earned him eight years in the gulags.

He survived the gulags and a bout with cancer. In a prison hospital, he committed his life to Jesus Christ. His experiences formed the basis for such books as *Cancer Ward* and *The Gulag Archipelago*. Awarded the Nobel Prize for Literature in 1970, he was exiled from the USSR in 1974.

In 1978, he delivered the commencement address at Harvard University. In that address, he not only condemned the totalitarian oppression of the Marxist Soviet system, but also criticized America for its materialism, vulgarity, and lack of courage in confronting evil. He reserved some of his most pointed criticism for the American press:

The press can both stimulate public opinion and miseducate it. Thus we may see terrorists heroized; or secret matters, pertaining to one's nation's defense, publicly revealed; or we may witness shameless intrusion on the privacy of well-known people under the slogan: "everyone is entitled to know everything." But this is a false slogan, characteristic of a false era. People also have the right not to know, and it is a much more valuable one: The right not to have their divine souls stuffed with gossip, nonsense, vain talk.[16]

The state of journalism is far worse today than when Solzhenitsyn delivered those words. We are awash in superficiality and misinformation. We see terrorists being portrayed as heroes. Throughout the Iraq and Afghanistan Wars, we saw newspapers scurrilously publishing national defense secrets on the front page. The media's wide-scale invasion of privacy made voyeurs of us all, and yes, that flickering plasma screen has indeed stuffed our souls with gossip, vanity, and much, much worse.

Whether in print or broadcast form, this thing that we call "the news" has manipulated our emotions—and stunted our thinking. While filling our eyes with images and our minds with useless information, it has not brought us closer to the truth.

The Bible in the Dustbin

In other parts of the world, we see the opponents of Christianity strangling freedom of speech, religion, and the press. Today, Canada conducts trials called Human Rights Tribunals that do not operate under the standard rules of the civil and criminal courts. The tribunals investigate, prosecute, and hand down verdicts in cases involving speech that offends minority groups.

Canadian-born journalist Mark Steyn has been a defendant before these tribunals because complaints were lodged by the Canadian Islamic Congress in multiple jurisdictions: the Canadian Human Rights Commission, the Ontario Human Rights Tribunal, and the British Columbia Human Rights Tribunal. All three complaints were directed at an October 2006 article Steyn wrote for *Macleans*, "The Future Belongs to Islam." The purpose of filing the complaint in multiple jurisdictions was to harass Steyn and his publisher—and to send a warning to other journalists and publications: Don't offend us or we'll come after you—and it will cost you a fortune to defend yourself.

The Ontario tribunal rejected the complaint on the basis that it did not have jurisdiction. The Canadian Human Rights Commission ruled in Steyn's favor in June 2008, and the British Columbia tribunal reached a similar ruling in October 2008.[17]

James Allan, law professor at the University of Queensland, Australia, writing in *The Australian*, offered a bleak assessment of the state of free speech in Canada:

> Here is a little-known fact about Canada: It is today a country where you can say or write things that are true and yet still be brought before a tribunal.
>
> That tribunal can fine you; it can order you to pay money to the people who complained about your words; it can force you to issue an apology; it can do all three.
>
> That's not all, though. The people who complained will not need to hire a lawyer. Their costs will be picked up by the state, by the taxpayers.
>
> You, on the other hand, will have to hire a lawyer to defend yourself. And there will be no award of costs at the end, so that even if you win, you will still be out of pocket to your lawyers tens of thousands of dollars....
>
> In the Steyn case, what the Canadian Islamic Congress is objecting to are quotations Steyn used. They are quotes of what Muslim leaders have said. So the purported grievance is that a writer is quoting one of their fellow religionists, and that quote (though true) might in the minds of those ideologues staffing these tribunals expose someone to hatred, even though in fact there is not a scrap of evidence that this has actually happened.[18]

Even though these tribunals ruled in favor of Mark Steyn and *Maclean's*, the Canadian Islamic Congress achieved its goal: In the future, Canadian writers will think twice about speaking the truth about militant Islam. Even though Mark Steyn wins, free speech loses.

In the Australian state of Victoria, two Christian evangelists, Daniel Scot and Danny Nalliah of Catch the Fire Ministries, were charged with a crime under Victoria's Racial and Religious Tolerance Act after a complaint was lodged by Islamic activists. The Muslims claimed Pastor Scot's seminar on "Jihad in the Qur'an," which encouraged Christians to evangelize Muslims, incited "hatred, contempt, and ridicule" against Islam. The pastors were found guilty and required to post repentant statements on their website and in newspaper ads (at a cost of around $68,000). They were also required to make no similar statements in the future—or risk more severe penalties.[19]

In Birmingham, England, two U.S.-born Christian evangelists were stopped by police for handing out Christian tracts in a Muslim neighborhood. The police told the evangelists that attempting to convert Muslims is a "hate crime." If members of the Muslim community physically attacked the evangelists, the evangelists themselves would be held responsible, not their attackers. "If you come back here and get beaten up," one police officer said, "well, you have been warned."[20]

Also, in England, Muslim attacks on Christian churches are becoming increasingly common. The Rev. Michael Ainsworth was attacked and beaten by three Muslim youths in his own East London churchyard. One reporter said that Muslim immigrants are intent on turning East London into a "no-go area for Christians." The British government, out of political correctness, has turned a blind eye to hate crimes against Christians. We will see more and more of these abuses as the Muslim presence in the West continues to grow—a silent, subtle, but effective form of jihad.[21]

The news media has largely under-reported these sorts of incidences, because to report on Muslim attacks against Christians would be "insensitive" and "intolerant." Feelings trump reason, and multiculturalism trumps Christian culture. The news media does not want to offend the feelings of Muslims, so the media has sacrificed objectivity and impartiality in favor of the multicultural agenda.

The extent to bias in British media was demonstrated in 2006 when reports emerged about an "impartiality summit" of executives of the British Broadcasting Corporation. The *Daily Mail* reported that, during the summit, BBC executives admitted that the broadcasting corporation is "dominated by trendy, Left-leaning liberals who are biased against Christianity and in favour of multiculturalism."

For example, BBC executives admitted that they would "let the Bible be thrown into a dustbin on a TV comedy show, but not the Quran, and that they would broadcast an interview with Osama Bin Laden if given the opportunity." The executives also "admitted the corporation is dominated by homosexuals and people from ethnic minorities, deliberately promotes multiculturalism, is anti-American... and more sensitive to the feelings of Muslims than Christians." The *Daily Mail* quoted one "veteran BBC executive" as saying that the bias is "so deeply embedded in the BBC's culture, that it is very hard to change it."[22]

Fairness Versus Freedom

We in the West are so intent on being tolerant and politically correct that we are acquiescing to our own destruction, the loss of our freedoms, and the subversion of our government, our media, and our culture. We don't want anyone to accuse us of being intolerant of Muslims. We don't want anyone to accuse us of "hate speech" by speaking up for our faith, our freedoms, our Constitution, and our way of life. We have elevated feelings over reason—and in the process, we are destroying the soul of Western civilization, along with our Bill of Rights.

Today, religious media remains largely free in the U.S.—but that could soon change. Many leaders in the Congress and throughout our society are calling for a return of the Fairness Doctrine, the "equal time" policy that was abolished by the Federal Communications Commission in 1987. Why was it abolished? Because the Fairness Doctrine killed free speech.

This policy could soon be re-imposed by congressional legislation or even through changes in FCC policies. The result: Christian broadcasters would be required to hand over a portion of their airtime to atheists, pagans, Satanists, and anyone else who disagreed with the Christian message. It would mean the end of Christian broadcasting—and the end of the First Amendment as we know it.

Chad Groening, a news anchor with American Family News Network, reports that the appointment of a "diversity czar" at the FCC signals a serious threat to free speech over America's airwaves. Groening says that the "diversity czar," Mark Lloyd, may be planning to achieve the goals of the Fairness Doctrine—the regulation of content on talk radio—by a "backdoor" method. Before being appointed to the FCC, Lloyd was a senior fellow at the Center for American Progress where he coauthored a document, "The Structural Imbalance of Political Talk Radio." Seton Motley of Media Research Center has called that document "a roadmap for liberal activists to use the FCC to threaten the licenses of stations with whom they do not agree politically." This would result in "shutting down conservative Christian talk radio."[23]

For example, if I preached a radio or TV message which cited the Bible's stance on homosexuality—even though it was presented in the context of God's unconditional love for all people, including homosexual people—a gay rights organization could demand equal time to offer an opposing view. The station carrying my program would have to provide that airtime free of charge or risk losing its broadcast license. Activists would target every radio or TV preacher and swamp those stations with complaints and demands. Inevitably, the broadcast stations would say, "We don't need this hassle," and simply do away with religious programming altogether.

And Christian broadcasting would pass into history.

Again, we see emotional appeals rather than reason and sound principles being used to decide the matter. Some on the left say, "It's not fair that there are more conservatives than liberals on the radio." By focusing on so-called "fairness," they use an emotion-laden word to short-circuit reason and logic. After all, no one wants to be seen as opposing "fairness."

But is it fair to use the power of the federal government to determine the content of speech on the public airwaves? Not according to the First Amendment: "Congress shall make no law... abridging the freedom of speech, or of the press." The First Amendment does not guarantee *fairness*. It guarantees *freedom*. The framers of the Constitution understood that there can be no fairness without freedom. If you take away freedom in the name of "fairness," you take away fairness as well.

So if you hear politicians or media pundits advocating so-called "fairness" in the media, I hope you will speak up on behalf of freedom and the First Amendment. I hope you'll write a letter to the editor, or phone your representative, or call that local talk show—while you still can.

Rattling the Gates of Hell

In January 2010, after the revelation of golfer Tiger Woods' multiple infidelities, Fox News commentator Brit Hume offered this suggestion to Woods: "The extent to which he can recover seems to me to depend on his faith. He's said to be a Buddhist; I don't think that faith offers the kind of forgiveness and redemption that is offered by the Christian faith. So my message to Tiger would be, 'Tiger, turn to the Christian faith and you can make a total recovery and be a great example to the world.'"[24]

A storm of criticism erupted in the wake of Brit Hume's comments. The following night Hume appeared on *The O'Reilly Factor*, and host Bill O'Reilly asked him what kind of response he had received. Hume smiled and replied, "It's always been a puzzling thing to me. The Bible even speaks of it. You speak the name of Jesus Christ... and all hell breaks loose."

Mr. Hume is exactly right. His remarks did indeed rattle the gates of hell. They also had an unsettling effect on the American media. Tom Shales, the TV critic at the *Washington Post*, was distraught. He demanded that Hume apologize for having "dissed about half a billion Buddhists" by saying that Buddhism does not offer forgiveness and redemption as Christianity does.[25] But Hume didn't "diss" anyone. He merely stated a fact that any good Buddhist would agree with: Buddhism does not offer forgiveness and redemption because Buddhism does not recognize the concept of sin.

On MSNBC, *Countdown* host Keith Olbermann wildly mischaracterized Hume's gentle words as an attempt to "force" and "threaten" Woods into converting to Christ. Olbermann said, "Brit Hume has tried to force Tiger Woods into becoming a Christian," and later referred to Hume's "bizarre on-air attempt to threaten Tiger Woods into converting to Christianity."[26]

All across the leftist and secularist media, pundits criticized and mocked Britt Hume for expressing his faith in Christ, and for commending his faith to a famously troubled man. To his credit, Mr. Hume seemed unruffled by the media firestorm his words provoked—and he cheerfully declined to back away from those words. In so doing, he set a good example for us to follow.

Condemning and ridiculing those who express their Christian beliefs, distorting their words and demanding apologies—it's all just another way of tearing down the crosses in our culture. The secularists who jeered and mocked Britt Hume for his thoughtful and respectful advice to Tiger Woods will never be satisfied until all the crosses are gone, until no one dares to speak the name of the One—Jesus Christ—who died on the cross.

Respect your freedom to speak out for your faith. Never back down or apologize for speaking the truth. Exercise your freedom of speech and your freedom of religion. You never know how much longer that freedom may last.

Chapter Four

Restoring Sanity to the Government

In May 2010, a group of students and parents from the Wickenburg Christian Academy in Arizona gathered on the steps of the Supreme Court building in Washington, D.C. The teacher snapped a picture, then led the group down the steps and off to one side, to avoid blocking the steps. The students gathered in a circle and began praying for the Court and for their country.

Within moments, a police officer strode up and ordered them to stop praying. When the teacher, Maureen Rigo, asked why, the officer said that the students were violating the law and would have to pray elsewhere. "I'm not going to tell you that you can't pray," he said. "You just can't pray here."

So the group—fifteen students from Ms. Rigo's American History class plus seven adults—moved toward the street. They literally stood in the gutter to continue praying because their government said they could not pray in the shadow of the Supreme Court itself.

Later, Ms. Rigo used the incident as a teaching opportunity. "We do a long study on the U.S. Constitution," she told Fox Radio News correspondent Todd Starnes. "We talked about... the right to freedom of speech, the right to freedom of religion. We have the right to peaceful assembly. We have the right to due process of law. We feel like all of those things had been denied us there."[1]

The following month, a group of high school students from the Young America's Foundation visited the Lincoln Memorial in Washington, D.C. As they stood before the great statue of Abraham Lincoln, one student was moved to sing the national anthem. The other students joined in—but as soon as they began singing, an officer of the U.S. Park Police ran over to the students and shouted, "Stop singing!"

The officer proceeded to tell the surprised students that singing the national anthem in front of the Lincoln Memorial was a violation of federal law. Singing constituted a "demonstration" and all demonstrations at that location had to be "completely content neutral." Apparently, our government considers the content of "The Star-Spangled Banner" to be controversial.

The students looked at each other—then, without a word of discussion, they continued singing the national anthem. Todd Starnes called it "an impromptu form of civil disobedience." The Park Police officer made no further attempt to stop them. As one of the students later explained, "We just wanted to pay respect to our nation—in our capital."[2]

The irony of these instances seems totally lost on the misguided police officers—who interpreted the laws in a way that makes it a crime to pray and sing the national anthem around the marble pillars of our government. Isn't the Supreme Court the very institution which *defends* our First Amendment right to free speech and the free exercise of religion? Why are students forbidden to pray there? Wasn't Abraham Lincoln a president who literally gave his life to preserve freedom and the Union? Why are students forbidden to sing the national anthem at the site of his memorial?

These incidents in our own nation's capital are enough to make you wonder: Do we still live in America, "the land of the free and the home of the brave"? Has our government lost its mind?

The Face of Your Future

In February 1990, a young Florida woman named Terri Schiavo suffered cardiac arrest, resulting in irreversible brain damage. She was institutionalized and her life was maintained by a feeding tube. After eight years, her husband, Michael Schiavo, petitioned the court to remove her feeding tube—and starve her to death.

The husband maintained that Terri was in a comatose condition called a "persistent vegetative state." Though she was awake and her eyes would open, her husband claimed she was unthinking and unaware of her surroundings. Her parents, Robert and Mary Schindler, opposed the husband's petition, arguing that their daughter showed signs that she was conscious and aware.

For seven years, a highly publicized legal battle raged over the fate of Terri Schiavo. By March 2005, her case had gone through numerous state and federal courts, and the U.S. Supreme Court had four times refused to hear the case. Judges ordered the feeding tube removed, then reinserted, removed, then reinserted.

On March 18, 2005, a judge ordered the tube removed a third and final time. For nearly two weeks, Terri Schiavo received no food and no water. She was deliberately starved and dehydrated to death by court order.

Starvation is a terrible and painful way to die. The body fights to stay alive and over time it begins breaking down its own tissues—first the fat, then the muscle, and finally even the organ tissues—to keep the vital heart muscle and nervous system alive. Vitamin deficiency produces painful skin lesions and other symptoms of pellagra and anemia. At first, there's raging thirst, with cracking lips and a dry tongue. Eventually the victim becomes too weak to sense thirst. Swallowing becomes unbearably painful. The body wastes away.

We would not execute a mass murderer in such a horrible way. Anyone who treated a dog so inhumanely could spend years in prison. Yet that is the death sentence the court imposed on Terri Schiavo.

This woman did not need "heroic" measures to sustain her life. She did not require a respirator, surgery, transplants, dialysis or any other costly or extreme procedures. She just needed nourishment and water, administered through a feeding tube. The court decided that she wouldn't want to live such a life. But did the court consider whether she wanted to die such a death? It would have been kinder to kill her by lethal injection or even a bullet—but that, of course, would be murder. Somehow, a husband and a judicial system were able to convince themselves that death by deliberate starvation was somehow morally different from murder. Yet, if we think rationally and logically about the matter, it becomes clear that the hand that removes the feeding tube is no different than the hand that injects the poison or the hand that fires the gun—except the hand that killed Terri Schiavo was far crueler.

On March 31, 2005, after thirteen days of slow starvation, Terri Schiavo died in a Florida hospice care facility. She was forty-one.

Her death is proof that our society has lost its mind. We are, as a culture, voluntarily surrendering our ability to think rationally. It's not that we are merely ignorant. We have all the information we need to make informed decisions. In Terri Schiavo's case, we know what death by starvation is. We understand that her death was an act of judicial cruelty.

But our judges willfully set aside their ability to use that information, to analyze it and draw conclusions from it, and to make wise, humane decisions. Instead, they maintain a smug indifference to the truth so that they can carry out experiments in social engineering, disposing of "inconvenient" people like Terri Schiavo on an unproven theory that "she wouldn't want to live this way."[3]

In years to come, as the Baby Boomers trade in their BMWs and SUVs for walkers and wheelchairs, will they become just as "inconvenient" to society as Terri Schiavo was—only vastly more numerous. The judges, bureaucrats, legislators, and social engineers will continue to build their brave new world on the corpses of the weak and helpless.

So look into the face of Terri Schiavo as she suffers and dies. Is this the face of your future?

Losing Our Collective Mind

In our entertainment and news media, our universities, and our political institutions, experts and opinion leaders tell us that feelings are all that matter, that we should set aside reasoning and objective truth. If we apply Christian principles to any situation, the self-appointed "thought police" accuse us of being "rigid," "judgmental," and "self-righteous." They say, "Truth is in the eye of the beholder," or, "Who's to say what's right and what's wrong? What's true for you isn't necessarily true for me!"

Back when reason and objective truth were respected in our culture, people would ask, "What do you *think* about this issue?" Today, people ask, "How do you *feel* about this issue?" That is not a small distinction. These are two very different questions, and the "How do you feel" question reflects the fact that feelings trump thinking in our society today. Crucial, life-and-death issues are increasingly being decided by emotional appeals instead of rational principles and objective truth:

"Terri Schiavo wouldn't want to live that way. She's better off dead." So we kill her.

"Every child should be a wanted child." So we do "unwanted" children a favor and abort them.

56

"We have to save the planet and stop global warming!" So we hastily adopt a lot of "green" regulations which harm the economy, hurt the poor, and make environmental problems worse.

"It's not fair that some are rich and others poor." So we declare "war on poverty" and wage that "war" decade after decade—and poverty only increases. In fact, America's "war on poverty" is a prime example of why emotion-based "solutions" to social problems only compound the problem.

Let's start with a premise: We want society to be compassionate toward people in need. We all support a social "safety net" for people who are either going through temporary financial difficulties or are unable to provide for themselves.

But America's "war on poverty," declared by President Lyndon Johnson in 1964, goes far beyond a "safety net." And the "war" has backfired, producing more of the very poverty, crime, illegitimacy, and suffering it was intended to cure. In a 2004 column, economist Thomas Sowell of the Hoover Institution wrote:

> Never had there been such a comprehensive program to tackle poverty at its roots, to offer more opportunities to those starting out in life, to rehabilitate those who had fallen by the wayside, and to make dependent people self-supporting. Its intentions were the best. But we know what road is paved with good intentions.
>
> The War on Poverty represented the crowning triumph of the liberal vision of society—and of government programs as the solution to social problems.... While some good things did come out of the 1960s,... so did major social disasters that continue to plague us today. Many of those disasters began quite clearly during the 1960s.[4]

Dr. Sowell describes the good intentions—and disastrous results—of the "war on poverty." To attack the crime problem in the slums, the LBJ administration tore down inner-city slums and built brand-new government housing projects. Problem: The housing projects turned into slums again. Poverty and crime persisted. Eventually the projects had to be torn down as well.

Prior to LBJ's "war on poverty," Dr. Sowell observes, rates of violent crime, teen pregnancy, and sexually transmitted diseases had been declining. After 1964, those rates skyrocketed. The once-strong African-American family structure, which had endured centuries of slavery and segregation, could not withstand the "compassion" of the "war on poverty." The new welfare state actually created subsidies for unwed pregnancy; the state cut payments to mothers and children if Dad was in the picture—so Dad left. Welfare, once viewed as a "safety net," became a way of life for many.

One of the most destructive effects of the "war on poverty" was on children born out of wedlock. According to the National Center for Health Statistics, 20 percent of African-American children and 2 percent of white children were born out of wedlock in 1954. By the time the "war on poverty" was announced in 1964, those rates were up slightly—25 percent for African-American children and more than 3 percent of white children.

But after less than two decades of the "war on poverty," it was clear that something had gone disastrously wrong with the American family. By 1982, the illegitimacy rate among African American families had zoomed to 58 percent; the illegitimacy rate among the white families had also soared, to 12 percent. Just fifteen years later, in 1997, the illegitimacy rate was 69 percent among African-Americans and 26 percent among whites.[5]

The welfare state *encouraged* illegitimacy, and the rising illegitimacy rates generated more unwed pregnancy, poverty, and crime. A report by the nonpartisan American Enterprise Institute for Public Policy Research observed:

> When a large proportion of the children in a given community grows up without fathers, the next generation, especially the young males in the next generation, tend to grow up unsocialized—unready to take on the responsibilities of work and family, often criminal, often violent. The effects of absent fathers are compounded by the correlations of illegitimacy with intellectual, emotional, and financial deficits among the mothers that in turn show correlations with bad parenting practices.[6]

Over the past four and a half decades, problems of illegitimacy, poverty, and crime have become institutionalized in our society. We have created a self-perpetuating underclass that has expanded, generation by generation. The idea that we could solve poverty by writing a monthly check to the poor only produced more poverty and broken families. Our well-intentioned programs trapped American families in a vicious cycle of dependency. Our so-called "compassion" was nothing but mindless cruelty.

According to an August 2008 report by the Cybercast News Service, "Since the 'War on Poverty' began in the 1960s under President Lyndon Johnson, more than $9 trillion has been spent to end poverty in the United States."[7] Do you have any idea how much $9 trillion is? One trillion is a million times a million. Harry G. Shaffer, professor emeritus of economics at the University of Kansas, pictures a trillion dollars this way: "A million dollar bills, laid end to end, would just about cover the distance from New York to Philadelphia; a billion would span the earth four times around the equator; but a trillion dollars would stretch more than 200 times to the Moon and back."[8] Nine trillion dollars is an inconceivable sum of money—more than all the money spent on every war America has fought, from the Revolutionary War until today.[9]

Despite the bipartisan welfare reform bill passed by the Republican Congress and signed by a Democratic president in 1996, the welfare state—and the problems of dependency, illegitimacy, and crime that result from it—continue to grow. Our caring, compassionate, feelings-oriented society continues to fund the destruction of families and the blight of our inner cities. We continue to fight a war on poverty we have already lost.

The solution to poverty comes from private and religious charities, and from the caring acts of people of faith. Authentic compassion does not come from government bureaucrats and government checks.

On one social issue after another, from the right to life to the war on terror to the environment to the war on poverty, we as a nation is losing our minds. We have ceased to be a society of reason; we have become a society led around by emotion.

"Just a Matter of Time"

Immediately after America was attacked by terrorists on September 11, 2001, emotions ran high. Americans were in shock. We couldn't get the images out of our minds—the airplanes slamming into the World Trade Center towers, the billowing flames, the doomed people jumping out of skyscraper windows, the collapsing towers, the ghost-like survivors covered in ash and fleeing Ground Zero, the gaping hole in the side of the Pentagon building, the burned scar in a Pennsylvania field.

After the attacks, we were united in our grief and resolve. Even the news media responded with support for the War on Terror. The cable news network MSNBC put up a "wall of heroes" and invited viewers to send photos of their loved ones who were going off to war. In late November 2001, an ABC News/*Washington Post* poll found that 78 percent of Americans supported the War on Terror, including taking action against Saddam Hussein and Iraq. By August 2002, support for the war was still high at 69 percent—but it had clearly softened as emotions waned. By March of 2003, when the U.S.-led coalition invaded Iraq, support for war in Iraq stood at 64 percent.

During the summer of 2003, sensational scandals involving NBA star Kobe Bryant and pop star Michael Jackson took attention away from the war. MSNBC quietly removed its "wall of heroes" and began reporting negatively on the war effort. By December 2004, public support for the war dipped to 39 percent—and would continue to fall thereafter.[10]

We quickly forgot the sense of shock and anger we felt one September morning in 2001 when some 3,000 of our fellow citizens were senselessly murdered. We forgot the horror we felt when we tried to imagine their last moments. We lost interest and enthusiasm for fighting against evil. Our support waned because our support was largely emotion-based, not based on principle or commitment.

In my travels around the globe, I have spoken with many Muslim leaders and thinkers. One statement I have heard from them again and again is, "America cannot persevere in war. We Muslims are patient. It's just a matter of time before we win." Why are they so confident that they will defeat the West? "Americans," they say, "are ruled by their emotions. They are not committed to a cause. Their emotions will cool off, they will lose interest and demand an end to the war. The American people are weak, decadent, and ruled by their passions. They have no stomach for fighting, as we do. That's why we will win."

They are largely correct because they get most of their views on the West from movies and the Hollywood culture—a culture led by its emotions and ruled by its passions.

Back in the Cold War years of the early 1980s, I wrote extensively, warning that Islamic fundamentalism posed a greater danger to Western civilization than Communism. I often wondered what it would take to wake up our Western culture from its slumber.

Then came the horror of September 11, 2001. How we all grieved and wept! We saw all Americans, regardless of political party, joining in unity and a common purpose. I thought, "Thank God! The nation is finally waking up to the threat from fundamentalist Islam! Americans finally realize that we cannot ignore the advance of extremism."

But that hope was short-lived. The images of 9/11 did indeed wake people up—for a while. The shock of the attacks stirred our emotions—temporarily. But the shock wore off, the emotions faded. We failed to truly understand political Islam. We pushed the snooze button—and we went back to sleep.

It wasn't long after the 9/11 attacks before another set of emotions began to emerge, again. There is a segment of American society whose default assumption is, "No matter what goes wrong in the world, blame America first." Many of these "blame America first" people are in government, but you also find them concentrated in our news media, in Hollywood, and in our universities. Whatever is wrong with the world—terrorist attacks on 9/11, insurgency in Iraq, starvation in Darfur, nuclear programs in Iran and North Korea, poverty in Latin America, or an ozone hole over Antarctica—it is America's fault. A decade after 9/11, anti-Americanism is fashionable once more.

A Mosque—But No Cross

In 2009, a group of investors purchased a building at 45-51 Park Place in lower Manhattan, just two blocks (about 600 feet) from the site of the 9/11 World Trade Center attacks. In fact, when the 9/11 terrorists flew United Airlines Flight 175 into Tower Two (the south tower), the plane's landing gear flew out of the building and struck the roof at 45-51 Park Place, penetrating the top two floors of the five-story building. In a real sense, the building is not *near* Ground Zero—it is *part of* Ground Zero.

The investment group was led by an Islamic Imam, a spiritual and community leader, named Feisal Abdul Rauf. Though Imam Rauf portrays himself as a moderate Muslim who is only interested in peace and understanding, he once told Ed Bradley on CBS *60 Minutes*, just weeks after the 9/11 attacks, "United States policies were an accessory to the crime that happened" on 9/11.[11] He also refuses to acknowledge that Hamas—an Islamic Palestinian organization that seeks to destroy the state of Israel—is a terror organization.[12] And he once said "Christians in World War II... bombed civilians in Dresden and Hiroshima."[13]

Months after purchasing the Park Avenue property, Imam Rauf and his organization, the Cordoba Initiative, announced plans to build an Islamic community center and mosque on that site, to be called Cordoba House. Opponents of the project quickly dubbed it "the Ground Zero mosque." Former Speaker of the House Newt Gingrich was among the first to oppose the plan, pointing out that the name "Cordoba" has an important historical significance. He wrote:

"Cordoba House" is a deliberately insulting term. It refers to Cordoba, Spain—the capital of Muslim conquerors who symbolized their victory over the Christian Spaniards by transforming a church there into the world's third-largest mosque complex.

Today, some of the Mosque's backers insist this term is being used to "symbolize interfaith cooperation" when, in fact, every Islamist in the world recognizes Cordoba as a symbol of Islamic conquest. It is a sign of their contempt for Americans and their confidence in our historic ignorance that they would deliberately insult us this way....

America is experiencing an Islamist cultural-political offensive designed to undermine and destroy our civilization. Sadly, too many of our elites are the willing apologists for those who would destroy them if they could.[14]

When a nationwide controversy erupted over the Ground Zero mosque, with public opinion tilting heavily against the project, New York's Governor David Patterson offered to assist developers in finding an alternate site for the mosque. The Cordoba Initiative replied that it intended to push ahead with the Islamic center near Ground Zero and that there were no plans to discuss the matter with the governor and his representatives.[15]

The developers of the Islamic center remained stubbornly committed to a project which offended the sensibilities not only of 9/11 families and New Yorkers, but of an overwhelming majority of all Americans. Why would Imam Feisal Abdul Rauf and the Cordoba Initiative remain so inflexible and insensitive to the feelings of Americans if, as they claim, they want to promote peace and understanding?

There can only be one answer. Mr. Gingrich's analysis is correct. Imam Rauf is committed to building the Mosque on this specific property because of its symbolic importance. The building at 45-51 Park Place was struck and severely damaged by parts of the hijacked airplane on 9/11. Building the Mosque on that site truly would symbolize *conquest*—not peace.

Even so, the president of the United States, the Speaker of the House, the New York state attorney general, and the mayor of New York City all spoke out in support of Cordoba House. What's more, in the very midst of a heated national debate over the Ground Zero mosque, the State Department announced it was sending Imam Rauf on a *taxpayer-funded* "goodwill tour" around the Muslim world. It is almost as if the U. S. government is deliberately poking its finger in the eyes of its own citizens.

I can't see into the hearts of the leaders who openly support the Ground Zero mosque, but I suspect that the reason they spoke out as they did was because of so-called "political correctness." The political correctness mindset comes from a misplaced desire to be thought of as "enlightened" and "broad-minded" and "tolerant." The commitment to political correctness, in many cases, is not so much a matter of genuine tolerance (after all, those who pride themselves on political correctness are rarely tolerant of public displays of the cross). Rather, such people feel an emotional need to be liked and admired by the intelligentsia, by academia, and by opinion leaders in the media and in the arts community—by all the "enlightened" people.

Writing in the *Ottawa Citizen*, two moderate Muslims, Raheel Raza and Tarek Fatah, penetrate the façade of political correctness surrounding the Ground Zero mosque, and expose the hidden Islamist agenda behind the Cordoba Initiative:

> New York currently boasts at least 30 mosques so it's not as if there is a pressing need to find space for worshippers.... We Muslims know the idea behind the Ground Zero mosque is meant to be a deliberate provocation to thumb our noses at the infidel. The proposal has been made in bad faith and in Islamic parlance, such an act is referred to as "Fitna," meaning "mischief-making" that is clearly forbidden in the Quran....
>
> Teary-eyed, bleeding-heart liberals... are blind to the Islamist agenda in North America.... Their stand is based on ignorance and guilt, and they will never in their lives have to face the tyranny of Islamism that targets, kills and maims Muslims worldwide, and is using liberalism itself to destroy liberal secular democratic societies from within.[16]

The phrase "teary-eyed, bleeding-heart liberals" gets to the heart of the issue. Liberals who support the Islamist agenda do so for emotional reasons, such as guilt—not because of reason and principle. Genuine tolerance and compassion are commendable qualities—but some people are so eager to be applauded for their politically correct "tolerance" and "compassion" that they forget to be compassionate toward the families of 9/11 victims. They forget to be tolerant and sensitive to the views of the majority. Those in the politically correct crowd are so desperate to win the approval of Muslims that they are opening up our nation to be destroyed from within.

Some would say that Muslims have a First Amendment right to build a mosque on private property in lower Manhattan. I would agree: As far as the Constitution is concerned, Muslims have that right—subject, of course, to the zoning and regulatory requirements of New York City.

But don't Christians have a First Amendment right to build a church on private property on lower Manhattan? Then why has St. Nicholas Greek

Orthodox Church—which was destroyed on 9/11—never been rebuilt? From 1922 until 2001, St. Nicholas Church stood as a landmark on Liberty Street. The church was completely obliterated by the collapse of Tower Two. The St. Nicholas congregation has been battling the Port Authority of New York and New Jersey for the right to rebuild its church for more than a decade. Mark Impomeni writes in *Human Events*:

> Trouble emerged after St. Nicholas announced its plans to build a traditional Greek Orthodox church building... topped with a grand dome. Port Authority officials told the church to cut back the size of the building and the height of the proposed dome, limiting it to rising no higher than the World Trade Center memorial. The deal fell apart for good in March 2009, when the Port Authority abruptly ended the talks....
>
> St. Nicholas Church's difficulty in getting approvals to rebuild stands in stark contrast to the treatment that the developers of the proposed Cordoba mosque have received.... The mosque is proposed to rise 13 stories, far above the height of the World Trade Center memorial, with no height restrictions imposed.[17]

Isn't that strange? A Christian congregation spends a decade arguing with bureaucrats for permission to rebuild a landmark church which had stood on private property for 79 years. For ten years, the government roadblocks the rebuilding effort. But if an Islamic cleric who blames America for 9/11 wants to build a mosque on the very site of the 9/11 attacks, government officials fall all over themselves to fast-track the project. The cross of St. Nicholas Church is gone, and a decade later the Port Authority is still in no hurry to replace it—but the Cordoba House mosque is expected to be built within a year.

Political correctness is irrational, it is unjust, and it is one of the reasons that the crosses are disappearing in America. Someday, when all the crosses are gone, we will look back and realize that they were removed not by the rational rule of law, but by the irrationality of political correctness. When the crosses are gone, replaced by the Islamic crescent and minaret, it will prove what the Muslim leaders told me is true: "Americans are ruled by their emotions."

An Informed and Enlightened Citizenry

In an April 2008 column, Dr. Thomas Sowell of the Hoover Institution noted, "One of the painful aspects of studying great catastrophes of the past is discovering how many times people were preoccupied with trivialities when they were teetering on the edge of doom." America, he added, was at just such a moment.

It was true—America at that time was preoccupied with a TV show about America's next singing idol, a novel about vampire romance, and tabloid questions about which actresses dated which rock stars. Even the primary election campaign, which was in full swing, seemed to revolve around trivialities and personalities—not around the real life-and-death issues facing our nation. Six months after Sowell wrote that warning, the nation's banking system collapsed, proving him right.

In that column, Dr. Sowell also said that the reason we tend to be preoccupied with trivialities is that we are easily manipulated by our emotions. "Many people," he writes, "seem to regard elections as occasions for venting emotions, like cheering for your favorite team or choosing a homecoming queen."[18]

An election is not a popularity contest. When we go to the polls, we are deciding the course of human events. These decisions need to be made thoughtfully, not emotionally. Choices must be based on truth and principle, not emotional manipulation. We can't allow the fate of humanity to be decided in a mindless way.

During the 2008 election, it became painfully obvious that the news media was actively trying to get Barack Obama elected president. The emotional bias in favor of candidate Obama was so obvious that NBC's *Saturday Night Live* ran a parody of the presidential debates in which fawning journalists asked such questions as, "Are you comfortable? Is there anything we can get for you?" and made such statements as, "I just really, really, really, really, really want you to be the next President!"[19]

Less than two weeks after the 2008 presidential election, the respected Zogby International polling organization surveyed Obama voters to test their knowledge of the issues and events of the campaign. The nationwide survey of 512 Obama voters found that only 54 percent of Obama voters answered at least half of the twelve multiple-choice questions correctly, and only 2 percent got perfect or near-perfect scores.

Zogby found that 94 percent of Obama voters correctly selected Sarah Palin as the candidate whose teen daughter was pregnant and 81 percent correctly identified John McCain as the candidate who wasn't sure how many houses he owned. "Obama voters did not fare nearly as well overall," wrote John Zogby, "when asked to answer questions about statements or stories associated with Obama or Biden—83 percent failed to correctly answer that Obama had won his first election by getting all of his opponents removed from the ballot, and 88 percent did not correctly associate Obama with his statement that his energy policies would likely bankrupt the coal industry." Moreover, "57 percent of Obama voters were unable to correctly answer that Democrats controlled both the House and the Senate."

Was the survey intended to prove that Obama voters were ignorant or stupid? Of course not. This poll is not an indictment of voters but of a journalistic community which is biased, lazy, dishonest, or all of the above. Documentary filmmaker John Ziegler, who commissioned the Zogby poll, explained, "This poll really proves beyond any doubt the stunning level of malpractice on the part of the media in not educating the Obama portion of the voting populace."[20]

As Thomas Jefferson once wrote, "An enlightened citizenry is indispensable for the proper functioning of a republic."[21] When citizens are kept in the dark about the views and objectives of the candidates, they are more likely to elect leaders who do not represent our will—and the republic can be led tragically off-course.

Emotional manipulation has always been part of the political process. Down through the centuries, politicians have used every trick in the book to reach the voters' emotions—stirring music, flags and fireworks, balloons and baby-kissing, and empty slogans. As Aristotle said in 340 B.C., "An emotional speaker always makes his audience feel with him, even when there is nothing in his arguments."[22]

"We the People" need truthful, complete, accurate information in order to make a wise and informed decision about the direction of the nation. That is why the Founding Fathers gave us the First Amendment freedoms of free speech and a free press. Only an informed and enlightened citizenry can choose wise leaders and hold them accountable.

A Duty Not to Vote?

Judd Gregg, a Republican Senator from New Hampshire, was nominated by President Obama to be Secretary of Commerce, but later withdrew due to policy differences with the president. In early 2009, while Congress was debating the $787 billion stimulus bill, Senator Gregg calculated the cost of the plan and said, "This is a massive movement of the government to the left. In five years it will double the public debt of the federal government. That means that, in five years, this administration is proposing running up more debt than has been run up in all the time since the beginning of the Republic."

Stop for a moment and consider what Senator Gregg is saying: Our government was proposing to spend more money than *all* other presidents, from George Washington to George W. Bush, *combined*. Think about the level of debt we are passing on to our children and grandchildren. Think about what will happen to our society when the government can no longer issue Social Security checks, Medicare checks, and welfare checks. Think about what will happen to America when we can no longer fund our schools, our military, or our police.

This is not a hypothetical scenario. This is our inevitable reality, our future—if our government does not stop spending us into oblivion. America is falling into a sinkhole of debt—and our elected leaders are doing nothing to stop it or even slow it down. Our government is making debt slaves of all of us, and our children, and our children's children.

The big-spending ways of our government should come as no surprise to anyone. We elect the government we want—and we tend to elect the government who promises us the most "goodies" from the public treasury. We vote our emotions, our greed, our laziness, our desire to get something for nothing from our government.

In his inaugural address in 1961, President John F. Kennedy said, "And so, my fellow Americans: ask not what your country can do for you—ask what you can do for your country."[23] Rarely, if ever, do politicians call on Americans to make sacrifices for their country anymore. Instead, politicians promise, "Vote for me, and I will open the vault at Fort Knox and shower you with benefits!" These appeals to our emotions, our greed, and our selfishness never fail, and that is why America is going bankrupt.

As citizens, we need to do our homework. We can't afford to unplug our intellects and hand over the world's most important job to the person who makes the most extravagant promises or delivers the most emotionally compelling speech. As a nation, we need to begin making wise decisions—before it's too late.

Voting is not just a right. It is a sacred trust—a solemn responsibility. As citizens of a self-governing society, we help shape the course of human history when we enter the voting booth. We have an obligation to cast our votes wisely and intelligently. If we allow ourselves to be swayed by emotion, we don't just let ourselves down—we break trust with God, with our nation, and with generations to come.

It's not wrong to engage our emotions and feel passionate about a cause or idea. But we need to vote with our heads as well as our hearts. We should take time to read the Declaration of Independence and the Constitution so that we truly know what it means to be an American. We need to be skeptical about the claims of politicians, pressure groups, and the news media. We need to do our homework about the candidates and the views they represent. If we fail to do the hard work of thinking for ourselves, then we allow others to do our thinking for us.

Shortly before the 2008 election, John Stossel hosted a segment of ABC News *20/20* entitled "John Stossel's Politically Incorrect Guide to Politics." He interviewed Andy Bernstein, co-founder of HeadCount, an organization which stages rock concerts in order to register young people to vote. Said Bernstein: "It is so imperative that this generation's voice is heard."

It sounds like a reasonable statement—but Stossel questioned Bernstein's assumption. He and his film crew went to a HeadCount concert and interviewed many young people, testing their knowledge. He asked them how many senators there are in the U.S. Senate. One young concertgoer said 12, another 64, and another guessed, "Fifty per state?" When Stossel asked what the Roe v. Wade decision was about, he received such replies as: "Segregation, maybe?" "Where we declared bankruptcy?" "What's Roe v. Wayne?"

Stossel concluded, "When people don't know anything, maybe it's their civic duty *not* to vote.... I'm not saying that the government should impose a litmus test. God forbid. I just want clueless people to find something else to do on November 4. Voting is serious business. It works best when people educate themselves."[24]

Now, I would *never* tell anyone not to vote. But we live in a dangerous world. The next election could determine whether we suffer a devastating terror attack, or tumble into another Great Depression, or trigger a nuclear Doomsday. It should disturb us to know that our elections are decided by people who are uninformed, misinformed, and easily manipulated by emotional appeals. It should frighten us to know that the future of our civilization is being determined by people who are utterly clueless about the issues—and even about the structure of their own government. As John F. Kennedy said in a 1963 speech at Vanderbilt University in Nashville, "The ignorance of one voter in a democracy impairs the security of all."[25]

If you don't understand the Constitution, the issues of the day, and the positions of the political candidates, then you should ask yourself: "Do I really belong in that voting booth?" After all, you may be canceling out the vote of a truly thoughtful, careful, knowledgeable voter.

I would never tell you not to vote. Instead, I'm pleading with you: Don't be swayed by emotional appeals. Use the mind God gave you. Engage the powers of your intellect. Do your homework—then do your part to preserve the heritage of freedom that was handed down to you at great cost.

Chapter Five

Restoring Sanity in the Classroom

Columnist and talk-show host Dennis Prager tells a story about his friend's son. The boy, age thirteen, was playing in a youth league baseball game. In the ninth inning, the boy's team was winning by a lopsided score of 24 to 7. The boy's dad, sitting in the bleachers, looked at the scoreboard and was surprised to see that the score had been changed. It now read 0 to 0.

After the final out, the dad went down to the field and asked an official if the scoreboard was broken. The reply: No, there was nothing wrong with the scoreboard. The coach of the winning team had asked the scorekeeper to change the score. He came to that decision after talking to some parents who were concerned that the boys on the losing team would have hurt feelings.

I ask you: Did the parents and the coach actually think that, by changing the scoreboard, the boys on the losing team would forget they had lost? I don't know about you, but when I was a boy, if someone had changed the score to spare my feelings, I would have felt even *more* humiliated! Better the pain of a good honest loss than be pitied.

Prager observed that the game was a microcosm of what is taking place throughout the American educational system: Feelings trump all other values, especially the values of truth, wisdom, character, and basic fairness. He writes:

> It is unwise to the point of imbecilic to believe that the losing boys were in any way helped by changing the score. On the contrary, they

learned lessons that will hamper their ability to mature.

They learned that someone will bail them out when they feel bad. They learned that they do not have to deal with disappointment in life.... They learned that their feelings, not objective standards, are what society deems most important....

At the same time, the boys on the winning team learned not to try their best. Why bother?[1]

Compassion has its place, of course, and we should always strive to be compassionate people. But when compassion or any other emotion prompts us to violate truth and fairness, then our compassion is corrupted and misplaced.

Education: Dumbed-down and Redefined

Where has all of this emphasis on feelings in education come from? Much of it has been deliberately engineered by education authorities over several decades. One such authority was Benjamin S. Bloom, "the father of Outcome-Based Education," who wrote in his 1981 book *All Our Children Learning*, "The purpose of education and the schools is to change the thoughts, feelings, and actions of students."[2]

Now, that is a startling statement. If I were asked to define education, I would say that education is the process of imparting knowledge, reasoning skills, and sound judgment so that students are intellectually prepared for a productive life. But Dr. Bloom believed it was the job of schools to meddle in the thoughts and emotions of students. Why did Dr. Bloom not even mention the purposes that most people associate with education—the teaching of knowledge and academic skills?

Ann Wilson, author of *Pavlov's Children*, a study of the impact of Dr. Bloom's theories on the education establishment in America, says that by the early 1990s, Bloom's educational model had "redefined what schools are for." The result is that schools now exist "to transform our culture by social engineering through psychological manipulation."[3]

Dr. Bloom's "outcome-based education" approach (also known as "standards-based education," "mastery education," or "performance-based education") has become the primary model for American education today. It may well be that we are seeing—and reaping—the impact of Dr. Bloom's theories in today's generation of college graduates.

According to *The New York Times*, literacy in English is declining among American college graduates at an alarming rate. In 2003, the Department of Education administered the National Assessment of Adult Literacy, which the *Times* called "the nation's most important test of how well adult Americans can read." It was the first time the test had been administered since 1992. The *Times* compared the findings:

In 1992, 40 percent of the nation's college graduates scored at the proficient level, meaning that they were able to read lengthy, complex English texts and draw complicated inferences. But on the 2003 test, only 31 percent of the graduates demonstrated those high-level skills. There were 26.4 million college graduates.

The college graduates who in 2003 failed to demonstrate proficiency included 53 percent who scored at the intermediate level and 14 percent who scored at the basic level, meaning they could read and understand short, commonplace prose texts.

Three percent of college graduates who took the test in 2003, representing some 800,000 Americans, demonstrated "below basic" literacy, meaning that they could not perform more than the simplest skills, like locating easily identifiable information in short prose.[4]

Grover J. Whitehurst, a Department of Education official in charge of overseeing the test, blamed the 9 percent drop in literacy among college grads on television and the Internet—but I would suggest that the fault may in fact lie with our education establishment. When we move away from imparting knowledge and reasoning skills, and we seek instead to "change the thoughts, feelings, and actions of students," this steep drop in literacy is a result we should *expect* to see.

What was Dr. Bloom's goal in seeking to "change the thoughts, feelings, and actions of students"? Simply this: Dr. Bloom's approach is directed at *changing and controlling what students believe.*

Feelings-based education seeks to break down the influence of a child's natural authority figures—parents and God—and to replace them with the authority of social engineers like Benjamin Bloom. And the way he seeks to do this is by teaching children, in effect, "Do not accept the rigid standards of right and wrong you were taught at home. Start with your own feelings, your own ideas, and build your own beliefs based on new ways of thinking—which we will introduce to you."

You may think that's an overstatement. But let me quote from another influential book by Dr. Bloom, published in 1964. The book is dense with jargon, and when reading these quotes, you need to remember that the word "affective" means "relating to, arising from, or appealing to the emotions." Dr. Bloom writes:

> The careful observer of the classroom can see that the wise teacher as well as the psychological theorist use cognitive behavior and the achievement of cognitive goals to attain affective goals.... In fact, a large part of what we call "good teaching" is the teacher's ability to attain affective objectives through challenging the student's fixed beliefs.[5]

Later, Dr. Bloom makes this telling observation: "The affective domain contains the forces that determine the nature of an individual's life and ultimately the life of an entire people."[6]

Now, let's translate this jargon into English: Dr. Bloom is telling us that a student's emotions and attitudes ("the affective domain") are the key to that student's life. If you can influence the emotions of an entire population of students, you can reshape and re-engineer an entire society. In Dr. Bloom's view, "good teaching" is teaching that uses the student's emotions to challenge (and ultimately change) the student's "fixed beliefs." A student's "fixed beliefs" are the beliefs he or she enters school with—beliefs that have been taught by the parents and the church.

Charlotte Iserbyt is a former senior policy adviser in the Department of Education during the Reagan administration. In her book, *The Deliberate Dumbing Down of America,* Iserbyt cites a myriad of examples to show that there has been a deliberate attempt to reshape our education system and manipulate the emotions and attitudes of our children. It is, she warns, a large-scale experiment in social engineering. Iserbyt quotes the testimony of a Maryland parent, Jacqueline Lawrence, before a subcommittee of the Senate Committee on Labor and Human Resources:

> Prior to the 1960s, American public schools placed major emphasis on the intellectual development of our children, on their mastery of basic skills such as reading, writing and mathematics. Competency in physics, biology, chemistry, and chronological factual history was required....
>
> Since the 1960s, academic standards have declined. Why? Quite simply, over the past twenty years our schools have not placed emphasis on academic achievement. There has instead been a shift toward psychological development and social adjustment of students in the affective domain, that is, their feelings, attitudes, and opinions. The shift began in 1965 with the passage of the Elementary and Secondary Education Act (ESEA).... Since 1965, billions of federal dollars have been allocated to educational theorists and curriculum developers to alter the course of public education.[7]

Some observers of public education saw this major shift in emphasis as far back as the early 1970s. Mary Thompson of the Republican Women's Federation warned in a speech on June 11, 1972: "Education itself has been redefined. Simply put, it has become the objective of education to measure and diagnose the child in order to prescribe a program to develop his feelings and emotions, values and loyalties, toward pre-determined behavioral objectives."[8]

The late Senator Sam Ervin from North Carolina once wrote, "If our society is to remain free, one man must not be empowered to change another man's personality and dictate the values, thoughts and feelings of another."[9] Today, however, we are seeing educators being empowered to change the personality, values, thoughts, and feelings of children.

The Bitter Fruit of the "Feelings Tree"

In their book, *The Dangerous Rise of Therapeutic Education*, Kathryn Ecclestone and Dennis Hayes of Oxford Brookes University in England tell the story of an eight-year-old girl who came home from school feeling distressed. Her problem: She didn't have a "worry" to write down. Every day, children would write down their "worries" and put them in the class "worry box." The teacher would then withdraw one of the "worries" from the box (they were unsigned and anonymous) and the children would sit around at circle time and discuss the "worry."

When this girl couldn't think of a "worry" for the "worry box," the teacher sent her home with an assignment to come up with a "worry" by the following day. It seemed that if the child didn't have a worry in the world, the teacher was determined to give her one! This is what the mindless focus on feelings is doing to our children.[10]

At another school, children gather in daily "nurture groups" around a "feelings tree." The students start their day by stepping up to the tree and choosing a paper "feeling" which represents their own emotional state. A child holds up the "feeling" and talks to the other children in the circle about why he or she feels that way. The aim of this exercise is to enable the children to develop "a vocabulary of feelings."

Other schools practice variations on this exercise. Some teachers have students make pictorial displays of their emotional state out of drawings of facial expressions or photographs clipped from magazines.[11]

Ecclestone and Hayes conclude that, beginning with the earliest years and going right up through high school and university levels, our Western educational system is producing a generation of "can't do students," young people who know how to discuss their emotions, but have not acquired knowledge and don't know how to think.

"Turning teaching into therapy is destroying the minds of children, young people and adults," Dr. Hayes told Alexandra Frean, education editor for *The Times* of London. "Therapeutic education promotes the idea that we are emotional, vulnerable and hapless individuals. It is an attack on human potential."[12]

One primary school teacher noted that the focus on students' emotions made the job easier in some ways: "At least we can talk to parents about a child's emotional and personal development when we can't find anything good to say about their child's academic progress."[13] Somehow, I find little comfort in the fact that the teacher's job is easier, while we are graduating a generation of students who have wonderful self-esteem, but cannot read their own diplomas.

The Unconstitutional God

This ill-conceived feelings-based corruption of education comes at a time when the spiritual well-being of our children is also under attack. A landmark 1962 Supreme Court case, *Engel v. Vitale*, declared prayer in public schools "unconstitutional." From that day until the present, it has been illegal for a teacher or school officials to lead prayer in an American public school.

The offending prayer, which was composed for the public schools of New York state, read: "Almighty God, we acknowledge our dependence upon Thee, and we beg Thy blessings upon us, our parents, our teachers and our Country." Students who wished to opt out were excused. Even so, the justices ruled 6 to 1 that this simple prayer violated the First Amendment.

What does the First Amendment say about religion? Simply this: "Congress shall make no law respecting an establishment of religion, or prohibiting the free exercise thereof...." That prayer expressed the most basic and common form of theistic faith, rooted in our nation's broad spiritual heritage, and did not reflect the doctrines of any particular sect. It did not remotely constitute "an establishment of religion."

The lone dissenting justice, Potter Stewart, tried to remind his colleagues of the many instances in our public life where we openly acknowledge God: the national motto "In God We Trust," the Pledge of Allegiance which affirms that we are "one Nation under God," and the Declaration of Independence, which declares our "firm reliance on the protection of divine Providence."

But Justice Stewart's sound reasoning did not prevail. On June 25, 1962, the Supreme Court banned even such simple, all-embracing acknowledgments of God—not only from the schools of New York state, but from every school in every state.[14] Somehow, our republic managed to survive the supposedly "unconstitutional" practice of prayer in schools for the first 184 years of its history. It is less clear that we will survive without prayer in the years to come.

When prayer was part of school life, students received a daily reminder that they lived in a culture that acknowledged the presence of Almighty God. The recognition that we live in a God-conscious, God-honoring society served to strengthen the fabric of our society. The banning of prayer, along with the later ban on displays of the Ten Commandments in schools, created a spiritual vacuum in our educational system. Though the high court intended to prevent the establishment of a state-sponsored religion in the schools, it actually established Atheism as the de facto state religion.

Justice Antonin Scalia put his finger on the source of conflict in our society in his dissenting opinion in the case of *McCreary County v. ACLU of Kentucky*, a case involving the display of the Ten Commandments in a Kentucky courthouse. Scalia wrote, "In the context of public acknowledgments of God there are legitimate *competing* interests: On the one hand, the interest of that minority in not feeling 'excluded'; but on the other, the interest of the overwhelming majority of religious believers in being able to give God thanks and supplication *as a people*, and with respect to our national endeavors. Our national tradition has resolved that conflict in favor of the majority." (Emphasis in the original.)[15]

When feelings trump principle, it seems that the only feelings ever considered are those of the vocal minority. Rarely is deference shown to the feelings of the religious majority—or to the actual wording of the First Amendment: "Congress shall make no law respecting an establishment of religion, or prohibiting the free exercise thereof."

If students were daily surrounded by reminders that they are part of a culture that acknowledges God, would life in our schools be different? Would we have had the rise in school violence, drug use, and bullying that we see today? Would the Columbine High School massacre and so many other school shootings have taken place? No one knows. But we can say this: There has been a steady and significant increase in all sorts of destructive behavior in schools ever since it became "unconstitutional" to mention God's name in the classroom. To avoid offending the vocal few, we have coarsened and corrupted an entire society.

The Islamic Simulation

In early 2002, while America was still reeling after the 9/11 terrorist attacks, a news story broke in Southern California that shocked the nation: Seventh-grade students at Excelsior Middle School in Contra Costa County were required to undergo a three-week course in which they essentially *became* Muslims. They took Islamic names, wore Islamic clothing, memorized verses from the Quran, practiced the Five Pillars of Islam (including fasting for Ramadan), and greeted each other with the words "Allah Akbar" ("Allah is Great").

At the end of the course, students were asked to talk about what they had learned and how their opinions about Islam had changed. A handout sheet advised, "*Be careful here.* If you do not have something positive to say, don't say anything!"

Students were required to only share opinions that endorsed the Islamic religion. Concerns or critiques were not welcome.

The news generated a firestorm of controversy, which school officials tried to quell. Byron Union School District superintendent Peggy Green said, "Dressing up in costume, role-playing and simulation games are all used to stimulate class discussion and are common teaching practices used in other subjects as well." Excelsior principal Nancie Castro added, "At no point do we teach or endorse religion." But parents weren't buying it.

In July 2002, the Thomas More Law Center filed suit to prevent the school from continuing its "Islamic simulation" program. Richard Thompson, the center's chief counsel, explained, "While public schools prohibit Christian students from reading the Bible, praying, displaying the Ten Commandments, and even mentioning the word 'God,' students in California are being indoctrinated into the religion of Islam.... Just imagine the ACLU's outcry if students were told that they had to pray the Lord's Prayer, memorize the Ten Commandments, use such phrases as 'Jesus is the Messiah,' and fast during Lent."

In December 2003, U.S. District Judge Phyllis Hamilton of San Francisco issued a 22-page ruling—*in favor of the school*. The Islamic indoctrination program would be allowed to continue. In her astounding opinion, Judge Hamilton declared that the program—despite its prayers, rituals, fasting, and memorization of Islamic scripture—was free of "any devotional or religious intent."

At the time, Judge Hamilton's decision seemed stunningly irrational— but irrationality is just part of a pattern with Judge Hamilton. Six months after deciding this case, she shocked the nation by overturning a federal law banning partial-birth abortion.

In the end, Judge Hamilton's decision in the "Islamic simulation" case was left standing by the activist Ninth Circuit Court of Appeals. The U.S. Supreme Court declined to hear the case. The same instructional materials are still in use in that school system today.[16]

But there's even more to this shocking story. The next twist begins with an incident in Washington, D.C.

In September 2003, a man named Abdul Rahman al-Amoudi was arrested at Washington Dulles International Airport, after arriving on a flight from London. British customs officials had caught him carrying $340,000 in sequentially numbered hundred-dollar bills. He later pled guilty to charges of illegal financial dealings with Libya and admitted involvement in an assassination plot against Saudi Crown Prince Abdullah. He was sentenced to twenty-three years in prison.

Who is Abdul al-Amoudi? What does he have to do with the "Islamic simulation" project in California?

Abdul al-Amoudi is a once-prominent Arab-American, the founder of the American Muslim Council and other Muslim advocacy groups. He met frequently at the White House with top officials of the Clinton and Bush administrations—including a 2001 meeting with senior Bush adviser Karl Rove regarding faith-based initiatives. After the 9/11 attacks, he even spoke at the Washington National Cathedral memorial service for the victims.

In an October 28, 2000 speech, he told a Muslim audience, "Either we do it now or we do it after a hundred years, but this country will become a

Muslim country. And I think if we are outside this country we can say 'Oh, Allah destroy America,' but once we are here, our mission in this country is to change it."

One of the ways he has been working to change America was by helping the Clinton administration draft a document called "Religious Expression in Public Schools," a set of guidelines distributed to every public school in America. When U.S. District Judge Phyllis Hamilton issued her ruling in favor of the "Islamic simulation" program, she relied upon those guidelines—drafted with the help of a Muslim extremist who seeks to turn America into a Muslim country.[17]

Comparing the Evidence

Let's be clear: I am *not* criticizing teachers. The vast majority of public school teachers are dedicated, caring professionals who chose educational careers out of a love for children and a commitment to learning.

I have spoken with many teachers who feel trapped by a system that is so bureaucratic and inflexible that it prevents them from doing the job they would like to do. They are doing the best they can in spite of demands from the government, a "politically correct" curriculum that is imposed on them, and apathetic parents who often do little to assist in the education of their own children. Teachers will tell you that the key to a child's performance in school is support in the home.

So I honor public school teachers and I recognize that they are performing nobly in the face of many obstacles. One of the best ways we can support our teachers is by opposing wrong-headed, feelings-based curricula that are destructive to the minds and souls of our children.

Take, for example, the issue of Intelligent Design in the schools. The question of how life began has generated a great deal of news coverage, litigation, and emotion in recent years. Most of the emotion, it seems to me, comes from people who want only one view presented in the public schools. Those who oppose the concept of Intelligent Design seem emotionally committed to silencing opposing views. They seem driven by fear. Otherwise, why fight so hard to keep opposing views from being heard?

The essence of learning is the willingness to explore all the evidence, to rigorously debate the hypotheses, to defend one's own position, to attack the weaknesses in the opposing position, to change one's mind when the evidence demands it, to maintain a spirit of honest inquiry—*and to follow the evidence wherever it leads*. Personally, I welcome the debate. I believe any fair-minded person should.

Some of the most respected scientists of our age are telling us that the universe shows unmistakable evidence of conscious, deliberate design. The late English astronomer Sir Fred Hoyle said, "I do not believe that any physicist who examined the evidence could fail to draw the inference that the laws of nuclear physics have been deliberately designed."[18]

Biologists John Maynard Smith of the University of Sussex and Eors Szathmáry of the Institute for Advanced Study in Budapest wrote in the scientific journal *Nature*, "It turns out that the physical constants have just the values required to ensure that the Universe contains stars with planets capable of supporting intelligent life.... The simplest interpretation is that the Universe was designed by a Creator who intended that intelligent life should evolve."[19]

And biologist Darrel R. Falk, author of *Coming to Peace with Science*, talks about his own science-based belief in a Creator: "I had one foot in the world of Christianity and the other in a world of secular knowledge. At that early stage of my life I thought that if I ever immersed myself in biological knowledge I would quickly slide down the slippery slope to agnosticism.... Yet, to my surprise, the early years of immersion in biology had no negative impact on my faith. I became increasingly impressed by the apparent design of life."[20]

Wouldn't an objective and open-minded thinker actually *want* his evidence to be compared side-by-side with the opposing evidence? If evolutionary evidence is sound, then logic dictates that those views would prevail. People generally seek to silence opposing viewpoints when they lack confidence in their own arguments.

The Screwtape Proposal

Many parents are fighting back against feelings-based education in the only way they can: They educate their kids at home. Home-schooling parents make a significant sacrifice, both in time and money, to educate their children. The reasons they generally give for home-schooling their kids are: (1) to prevent their children from being indoctrinated by false values; (2) to make sure their children receive a quality education, so that they are intellectually prepared to face the world; and (3) to provide the spiritual and moral instruction that public schools, by law, cannot offer. As Theodore Roosevelt once observed, "'To educate a man in the mind and not in morals is to educate a menace to society.'"[21]

But homeschoolers are under attack. In February 2008, a California court handed down a ruling which affected approximately 166,000 home-schooled children in the state. The court determined that all home-school parents had to have valid teaching credentials, or would have to put their children in public schools. Parents who violated the ruling risked prosecution and imprisonment. The court's decision amounted to a ban on home-schooling.

The ruling sent shock waves through California's home-school community—and indeed all across America. But it was applauded by one powerful interest group: the state's largest teacher's union. If most of those 166,000 children were forced back into the public school system, the state would have to hire more teachers, the ranks of the teacher's union would swell, and that would mean more money and more power for the union and its leadership.

Of course, the union's praise for the ruling was couched in terms of what's best for the children. "We're happy," said Lloyd Porter of the California Teachers Association. "We always think students should be taught by credentialed teachers, no matter what the setting."[22] I'm not saying Mr. Porter's concern for the students is not sincere, but there is clearly a conflict of interest: What's best for the union is not always what's best for kids. In this case, the ruling was clearly harmful to those 166,000 children—and it was an attack on parents' rights.

The ruling was the legal culmination of a long series of attacks on homeschooling. For example, in 2003, the *CBS Evening News with Dan Rather* ran a special report called "A Dark Side to Home Schooling," in which correspondent Vince Gonzales said, "Unlike teachers, parents need virtually no qualifications to home school. Not one state requires criminal background checks to see if parents have abuse convictions." The report went on to falsely suggest that home-schooled children are routinely abused, and it called upon the government to regulate home-schooling.[23]

We can clearly see the real agenda of home-school opponents in this revealing statement by atheist attorney (and former editor of *The Nation*) Paul Blanshard, writing in *The Humanist*: "I think that the most important factor moving us toward a secular society has been the educational factor. Our schools may not teach Johnny to read properly, but the fact that Johnny is in school until he is sixteen tends to lead toward the elimination of religious superstition."[24] If this man's thinking is any indication, then the social engineers of the brave new educational world don't really care about educating kids. Their primary goal is to impose atheism on society. Home-school families are on the front lines against these kinds of attacks against the minds of our children—and the battle is always fiercest on the front lines.

Studies have consistently shown that homeschoolers generally achieve beyond their grade level. A 1998 study involving more than 20,000 home-school students (based on the Iowa Tests of Basic Skills and the Tests of Achievement and Proficiency) showed that homeschoolers ranked 15 to 30 percentile points above the median for all students. Homeschoolers also score consistently higher than public school students on college entrance exams. A 2003 National Home Education Research Institute study showed that home-schooled young adults are better adjusted and more involved in serving their communities than their public-schooled peers.[25]

This brings us back to the 166,000 children affected by the February 2008 California ban on homeschooling. The good news for home-school families is that, on August 8, 2008, the Court of Appeal for the Second Appellate District in California reversed the earlier ruling. Homeschoolers are now free to continue their education.[26] But the war is not over. Expect the attacks to continue—and intensify.

As parents, educators, and concerned citizens, we must do whatever we can to restore sanity to our halls of learning. If our children are receiving indoctrination instead of education, if feelings-based therapy exercises have taken the place of genuine teaching and learning, then we must rescue our kids from the clutches of the social engineers.

In *Screwtape Proposes a Toast*, a 1959 sequel to *The Screwtape Letters* (1942), C. S. Lewis predicted the very condition to which public education has sunk. Lewis depicts the devil, Screwtape, explaining his plan to destroy young minds through a feelings-based public education system:

> The basic principle of the new education is to be that dunces and idlers must not be made to feel inferior to intelligent and industrious pupils. That would be "undemocratic." These differences between the pupils… must be disguised. This can be done on various levels…. At schools, the children who are too stupid or lazy to learn languages and mathematics and elementary science can be set to doing the things that children used to do in their spare time. Let them, for example, make mud-pies and call it modeling…. Whatever nonsense they are engaged in must have—I believe the English already use the phrase—"parity of esteem…"
>
> Of course this would not follow unless all education became state education. But it will.[27]

That is Screwtape's plan for removing the crosses from our world and from the hearts of our young people. We are living in Screwtape's world—a world in which nearly all education has become state education and the state education system has become focused on indoctrination through feelings-based methods.

We refuse to surrender to Screwtape and his ilk. We are fighting for the minds and souls of our children—and the battle rages on.

Chapter Six

Restoring Sanity in the Family

Dr. Ken Whitten is a pastor in Lutz, Florida. Interviewed by Orlando Magic vice president Pat Williams for his book *Souls of Steel*, Pastor Whitten told the story of how he and his wife Ginny raised their four children to live according to biblical principles, not according to their feelings.

"We homeschooled our children for several years," Pastor Whitten recalled, "preparing them and teaching them godly character traits before sending them out into the world. Our family standard is that our children may only watch movies rated G or PG. People sometimes asked what's wrong with a PG-13 rating. Sometimes nothing—but I've seen that what was once rated R is often rated PG-13 today."

One day, when the Whittens' oldest daughter Tara was a junior at Florida State University, her English professor told the class about the midterm exam the following day. The students would watch a movie, and then the class would be tested on the themes and issues in the film. The professor dismissed the class, and everyone filed out except Tara. She went up to the professor and asked what the film was rated.

"It's rated R," the professor said. "Why do you ask?"

"It's against my principles to watch R-rated movies," the young lady replied. "Could I please do something else for my midterm?"

"Tara," the professor said, "you're almost twenty-one, you're away from home, and it's time to grow up.... You choose: Watch the movie—or take a zero."

It was a tough choice. Tara would be the only student in the class not participating. She would be singled out as "weird" for clinging to her old-fashioned values and principles. Like the professor said, she was away from home. If she watched the movie, who would know or care? It would be so easy to go with her feelings and against her principles—but she was raised to follow her principles.

"I'll have to take the zero," she said. Then she turned to leave.

Astonished, the professor said, "Just a moment—what sort of alternate assignment did you have in mind?"

She suggested that she could write a paper.

The professor agreed—and assigned her a ten-page report on the subject of Tara's choice, due the following day.

That night, Tara wrote a ten-page paper on Proverbs 31 and titled it "A Godly Woman." She turned in the paper on time. A few days later, when the grades for the mid-term were posted, Tara was amazed to find that she received an A. In fact, she got the only A in the class.[1]

In a world where the crosses are rapidly disappearing, Tara Whitten planted her cross in her college classroom, and then stood immovably beside it. As Christian parents, having to battle a perverse culture for the souls of our children, we need to continually teach our kids to take a strong stand for their principles, even while everyone else obeys impulses and feelings. The survival of our families depends on our ability to cut through the fog of feelings while applying the clear, rational truth of God's Word to every situation in our lives.

Infected by Moral Relativism

As I talk to couples with troubled marriages, I find the most common reason they give for ending their marriage is, "I just *feel* that the marriage is over." Here again, feelings trump truth and values. These couples sound as if they are reciting lines from a soap opera. In some cases, perhaps they are. What happened to their marriage vows, their commitment to love each other "for better or worse, till death do us part?"

We are seeing a similar breakdown in parent-child relationships. Parents are increasingly operating on the basis of feelings instead of biblical principles and God's truth. Instead of raising their kids in the nurture and admonition of the Lord, parents have surrendered to their children's emotions—including childish anger and juvenile rage.

When God created the family, he had a special plan for this profoundly important element of human society. Christian author and social critic Rodney Clapp described God's vision for the family in his book *A Peculiar People*: "The Church sees family life as a great good. But the Christian family does not live, as some families in some cultures have, to perpetuate a name or preserve a nation-state by providing taxpayers and soldiers. The Christian family is defined by its action as an agent of the Church to witness to the truth of the kingdom of God."[2]

Does your family witness to the truth of the kingdom of God? Or does your family instead witness to the ever-shifting, feelings-based values of this dying world? If your family is living out God's vision for the family as an agent of God's changeless truth, then you and your family are in a distinct minority.

Americans have been ceaselessly brainwashed by moral relativism since the 1960s. The corrosive, ever-shifting values of our culture assault us from our TV screens, our movie screens, the Internet, the print media, and conversations with our peers. We have sunk to our necks in a swamp of moral relativism. So it shouldn't surprise us to learn that the vast majority of Americans reject the notion of absolute moral truth.

This fact is reflected in two nationwide surveys by the Barna Research Group of Ventura, California. These two surveys show that moral relativism has not only influenced the culture at large, but has actually infected the Christian church to a disturbing degree. In an article called "Americans Are Most Likely to Base Truth on Feelings," the Barna Research Group said it found that "less than one out of three born-again Christians adopt the notion of absolute moral truth. The surveys also found that few Americans turn to their faith as the primary guide for their moral and ethical decisions."

One survey was conducted among adults, the other among teenagers. In the total adult population survey—including both Christian and non-Christians adults—64 percent said that truth always depends on the person and the situation. Only 22 percent said that truth is always absolute.

The teen survey was even more lopsided. There, 83 percent of teenagers (both Christian and non-Christian) said that moral truth depends on the individual and the circumstances. Only 6 percent believe in absolute moral truth.

Clearly, we are seeing a shift in views, generation by generation. As the Barna Research Group article states, "It appears that relativism is gaining ground, largely because relativism appears to have taken root with the generation that preceded today's teens."

Christians who identified themselves as "born-again" were (as we would expect—or at least hope) more likely to believe in moral absolutes—but not by much. Among born-again Christian adults, 32 percent said they believe in moral absolutes, but among born-again Christian teens, that figure dropped to a mere nine percent. These findings have a profound impact on the way Americans in general, and born-again Christians in particular, make moral decisions and solve ethical problems. The article continues (the emphasis is mine):

> The surveys also asked people to indicate the basis on which they make their moral and ethical decisions... There was a clear pattern within both groups. By far the most common basis for moral decision-making was *doing whatever feels right or comfortable in a situation*. Nearly four out of ten teens (38 percent) and three out of ten adults (31 percent) described that as their primary consideration.[3]

How tragic! Most Americans, including most Christians, make their decisions on the basis of emotions, feelings, and impulses. They are living out the hedonistic motto of the drug-drenched 1960s: "If it feels good, do it!" When the founder of the Barna Research Group, George Barna, announced these findings in a public town hall forum, he noted that a significant number of Christians clearly believe that such actions as "abortion, gay sex, sexual fantasies, cohabitation, drunkenness and viewing pornography are morally acceptable." Barna went on to warn:

Just one out of ten of our country's born-again teenagers believe in absolute moral truth—a statistic that is nearly identical to that of non-born-again teens. Christian families, educators and churches must prioritize this matter if the Christian community hopes to have any distinctiveness in our culture. The virtual disappearance of this cornerstone of the Christian faith—that is, God has communicated a series of moral principles in the Bible that are meant to be the basis of our thoughts and actions, regardless of our preferences, feelings or situations—is probably the best indicator of the waning strength of the Christian Church in America today.[4]

The waning strength of the church is a direct reflection of the waning strength of the Christian family. With each succeeding generation, belief in absolute truth and absolute moral values diminishes more and more. Postmodernism and moral relativism have largely displaced biblical values and virtues in the minds of today's Christians, both young and old.

How can our children learn absolute values if parents no longer teach them? As values and virtues decline in our families and in our society, where will it all lead?

A God-centered Approach

A concerned father named Gil Reavill has written a book about the evils of pornography. Reavill warns that we Americans are failing our children by allowing them to be exposed—through TV, the Internet, the print media, and on and on—to "the world of commercial sex." Recalling all the sex-drenched media his middle-school-age daughter has been exposed to in her lifetime, he wrote:

> I recall suddenly feeling unworthy of the charge of being a parent.... I realized the degree to which we have failed our children. In a political sense, the young are powerless, voiceless, totally reliant on adults.... The boundaries of their world have been repeatedly breached, many times by people interested in making money and dismissive of all other considerations. All too often, our children are exposed to the

loud, frenzied, garish spectacle of adult sexuality. They get their faces rubbed in it....

I didn't like it. It made me mad.[5]

Those words sound as if they could have been written by a leading Christian spokesman—but Gil Reavill does not claim to be a Christian. In fact, he describes himself as having had a career *inside the commercial sex industry* since the early 1980s. His book is called *Smut: A Sex-Industry Insider (and Concerned Father) Says Enough is Enough.*

As a young man, Reavill saw himself as a rebel doing battle against a repressive society. Delighting in offending others, he wrote articles for *Playboy, Penthouse, Maxim,* and some publications with names I can't repeat here. What changed Gil Reavill's perspective on porn? Parenthood. It was as simple as that. Smut was merely a source of income before he became a father. But as his daughter grew up, he realized that pornography was a threat to her—a threat so pervasive it could not be avoided. He wrote:

I am thoroughly grounded with all the arguments against limiting, segregating, or censoring this kind of stuff, since I have used those arguments many times myself.

"If you don't like it, don't read it."

"If it offends you, change the channel."

"No one is forcing you to listen."

I am here to tell you that in America at the turn of the millennium, we have created a wholly original phenomenon.

The unchangeable channel.

The "off" switch doesn't work anymore. Our culture has been collectively hotwired.[6]

Understand, Mr. Reavill has not left the sex industry. He still writes for publications that are sleazy—*at best.* He doesn't want to eradicate or censor pornography. He thinks porn is a constitutional right, covered by the First Amendment. His plan is to "segregate" sexual expression away from "the public commons" in order to keep pornographers from shoving their wares in the faces of our children.[7] But keeping pornography "segregated" is not the answer. We need full-scale national repentance and a reaffirmation of God's truth.

Tragically, a large segment of our population—including the Christian community—chooses to obey feelings and base impulses instead of obeying the life-giving principles of God's Word. As a result, addiction to pornography is a spreading disease within many Christian families. A recent magazine report on Christians and pornography lists these troubling statistics:

> According to many Christian groups, pornography is a disturbing and increasing problem. A Promise Keepers survey found that 53 percent of its members consume pornography. A 2000 *Christianity Today* survey found that 37 percent of pastors said pornography is a "current struggle" of theirs. Fifty-seven percent called pornography the most sexually damaging issue for their congregations. A Barna Research Group study released in February 2007 said that 35 percent of men and 17 percent of women reported having used pornography in the past month.
>
> The pornography industry in the United States is indeed large. *Adult Video News*, an industry publication, estimates the industry's 2006 revenues at $13.3 billion. The U.S. is the world's largest producer and consumer of pornographic material. Porn websites draw 72 million visitors every month; more than 13,000 pornographic video titles are produced yearly.[8]

The Internet is a wonderful invention for communication, entertainment, retrieving information, conducting commerce, and many other valuable uses. But it is amazing to see how pornographers are always the first to exploit any new technology, from videotape to DVDs to the Internet to "mobile porn" over wireless Internet. Moral corruption is all around us—but that is no excuse for us as Christians to yield to our worst sexual impulses, to obey our temptations and our feelings instead of following our commitment to Christian character and biblical principles.

When we are tempted to surrender to lust instead of to God, there are some important facts we should call to mind. When we yield to pornography, we are aligning ourselves with the worst criminal elements in our society. Pornography generates billions of dollars for organized crime and it provokes criminal behavior. "Most child molesters admit that they consume hard-core porn on a regular basis," writes Charles Colson. "And those who create porn are now victimizing even the youngest children. Police who seize pornographic films and pictures note that they are seeing X-rated images of toddlers and even babies."[9]

The only true solution to an addiction to pornography is a complete surrender to God. All addicts, whether they crave alcohol or drugs or gambling or pornography, are actually trying to stuff something into a hole in their lives that only God can fill. This is why God-centered addiction programs like Alcoholics Anonymous are more successful than medical rehabilitation programs. A God-centered approach addresses the real issue in the addict's life: a hunger for God. Colson puts it this way:

> As surprising as it may seem, sexual addiction—like all addictions—represents a deep hunger for God. In their book, *The Sacred Romance*, Brent Curtis and John Eldredge point out that humans are designed for intimacy with God. Sometimes we allow the world, however, to drown out God's voice. But our need for communion with Him never goes away. Instead of seeking fulfillment in Christ, the addict tries to fill the emptiness with other things: pornography, an affair, or a fantasy life.
>
> As the authors put it, "We put our hope in… some form of immediate gratification, some taste of transcendence that will place a drop of water on our parched tongue…. [The addiction] attaches itself to our desire [for God] with chains that render us captive."[10]

Our Christian character either grows or diminishes according to the decisions we make and the temptations we resist—or yield to. The most important choices we make are often the ones we make in those private moments when no one is watching. Even a seemingly insignificant decision to say yes to a sinful impulse can produce a chain of circumstances leading to unbelievable suffering and destruction in our lives and families.

You may remember that a seemingly minor sin by King David ultimately led to his downfall. The Scriptures tell us, "In the spring, at the time when kings go off to war, David sent Joab out with the king's men and the whole Israelite army.... But David remained in Jerusalem. One evening David got up from his bed and walked around on the roof of the palace. From the roof he saw a woman bathing. The woman was very beautiful" (2 Samuel 11:1-2).

David was supposed to be out on the field of battle, leading his army. Instead, he remained behind in Jerusalem. As a result, he had too much time on his hands. Because he was the king, he didn't have to account to anyone for his time or his actions. So he got up one night, walked around the roof of his palace—and saw a woman bathing. It was the equivalent of a man of today, sitting at his computer, and stumbling onto a pornographic website. David stayed, he looked, and he lusted. He rationalized, "There's no harm in looking, is there?"

The moment he surrendered to his feelings and impulses, he set in motion a chain of circumstances and consequences that he could not foresee. He kept thinking about the woman and fantasizing about her. Then he acted on his fantasies and sent for the woman, whose name was Bathsheba. He committed adultery with her—and she became pregnant.

At that point, King David knew he had a scandal on his hands. He knew that Bathsheba's husband, a soldier named Uriah, was out on the battlefield and had been there for months. When Bathsheba gave birth, everyone would know the baby was not Uriah's. He could just see the headlines in the *Jerusalem Post*: "Bathshebagate Scandal: King Caught in Love Nest!"

So King David devised a cover-up plan. He tried to get Uriah to come home and spend the night with Bathsheba. But Uriah had such a strong sense of duty to his nation, his king, and the soldiers under his command that he refused to enjoy sexual relations with his wife while his men were out on the battlefield, enduring the rugged conditions of war.

King David's attempt at a cover-up was foiled. So he did the only thing he thought he could do to keep his sin from being exposed: He arranged for the murder of Uriah. At David's command, the men of Uriah's unit withdrew from him during battle, leaving him alone to face the enemy. So Uriah fell and died, betrayed by the king he nobly served.

The Scriptures tell us that "The thing David had done displeased the Lord" (2 Samuel 11:27). God sent Nathan the prophet to confront David about his sin of adultery and murder. When David's crime was exposed, he repented in deep sorrow—but by then, his sin had caused enormous harm and destruction that could never be undone. King David's seemingly "minor" sin—pausing to gaze at Bathsheba from the rooftop, pausing to lust for her—ultimately led to adultery, scandal, murder, and shame. It's not surprising that David's family fell apart.

As parents, we cannot lead our children to a place that we ourselves have not gone. If we want our kids to value absolute truth and biblical principles over feelings and impulses, then we have to live according to these principles ourselves. We cannot allow even "a little lust" or "a little pornography" to gain a foothold in our lives. The stakes are simply too high.

Bombarded by Messages

If we want to raise children who are strong in their faith, strong in character, and strong in principles and values, then we need to understand how they think and why they think that way. We need to acknowledge that the way they see the world is not the way we see the world. Our kids, even though they have grown up in our home, actually have at least one foot in a different culture: The youth culture.

Our children are growing up in a very different world from the one our generation knew. They are growing up with their brains plugged into a vast array of high-tech gizmos and gadgets, from iPods to cell phones. They are constantly socializing on Facebook and MySpace. They have brief attention spans and seem to need constant entertainment and stimulation.

The thinking of our kids is permeated with the postmodern worldview—a worldview in which feelings trump thinking. Heavily influenced by the popular media, the public school system, and their peers, they have probably bought into the mindset which says that all truth is relative. They may have even adopted the view that religious belief is purely a matter of personal preference.

Many young people would consider the Lord's words in John 14:6 to be "intolerant" of other religions. There, Jesus says, "I am the way and the truth and the life. No one comes to the Father except through me." Post-moderns generally reject the idea that there is only one path to God. They say, "You have your truth. I have my truth." The idea that there is *one* truth, *one* way, is simply not a part of the postmodern worldview.

You won't reach your kids and influence their thinking by trying to force them to see the world through your eyes. Instead, try to understand their world—then live your life in such a way, with such Christian grace and integrity, that your faith and principles will be attractive to them. Our kids are much more impressed by our walk than our talk.

The postmodern generation may not believe in objective truth, but they hate being lied to. They respect people who are honest and authentic. If your children know they can trust you, and that you will never betray them, you will build a powerful bond with your children—and you will earn the right to share your values with them.

It is often said that the postmodern generation prefers "narrative over proposition." That's just a fancy way of saying that young people today would rather hear stories than a bunch of dry facts. Who can blame them? Jesus certainly understands postmodern young people and the way they look at the world. He did most of His teaching in the form of stories called "parables." So, as you interact with your children, tell them stories—stories from the Bible, stories from your own experience, stories that you read in books or hear in a sermon, stories that make a powerful point about Christian virtue, biblical principles, moral purity, character, and truth.

Remember, your kids are being bombarded by messages that constantly attack the Christian faith and your family's values. They are being told on a daily basis that there is no such thing as objective truth. Feelings are all that matter.

It's normal and healthy, the world tells them, to yield to sexual temptation. The sex education they receive in their school probably promotes "safer sex," not purity and abstinence.

For many young people today, "morality" is nothing more than being "careful." They believe that there is nothing wrong with sexual behavior outside of marriage—as long as it is "protected sex." The psychological and spiritual ramifications of being sexually active at an early age never occur to them, because no one ever talks to them about it. Have you talked to your young people about these issues in their lives? If not, why not?

A 2005 survey by the Kaiser Family Foundation disclosed some troubling statistics regarding young people and the electronic media. The findings were examined in an article in the *Wall Street Journal*:

> When you factor in all the new gadgets and outlets—DVDs, videos, music, the Internet, computer video games, et cetera—the average kid gets 8 1/2 hours of exposure every day. The study, conducted among children ages eight to eighteen, says that more and more kids absorb this stuff in the privacy of their own bedrooms....
>
> The most startling revelation in the Kaiser report is that for a majority of kids there are no rules in the household about media use. Where there are rules, often they aren't enforced or they apply only to how many hours children watch TV, not to what they watch. This is strange. For example, the author of the Kaiser study, Vicky Rideout, notes that in an earlier survey, two-thirds of parents reported that they are very concerned about children's exposure to sexual and violent media content and that half said they believe such exposure affects their children's behavior a lot.[11]

Imagine—a child spending more than eight hours every day absorbing ideas, images, sensations, feelings, and worldly messages from the ever-present electronic media. Most parents express concern about that fact—but few parents are willing to *do* anything about it. They don't want to get their children upset. They don't want to deal with the emotional outbursts of their out-of-control kids. Here again, feelings trump principles and truth.

Do you know what your young people are doing online? Do you have the family computer out in a well-trafficked family area where your kids' online activities can be seen? Do you have filtering and monitoring software on your computer, so that you can always check on your kids' Internet activity? If your child has a computer in his or her room and can spend large amounts of unmonitored time online, I have a question for you: *What are you thinking?*

You may say, "But I don't want my child to think I don't trust him! I don't want to hurt his feelings or damage his self-esteem." If that is your position, then you are making a huge mistake. You are placing your child's feelings above principles—and above your biblical duty to raise your child in the nurture and admonition of the Lord.

That computer is a doorway to an entire world of soul-destroying images, messages, and ideas. If you allow your child to sit unmonitored and unobserved in front of a computer screen, you are throwing your child's soul to the wolves. The World Wide Web has many good things to offer young people—but it is also populated by Satanists, Wiccans, pornographers, sexual predators and every other vile thing that spews forth from the human imagination and the gates of hell. If you would not leave your child alone in the middle of a busy freeway, or in a brothel, or in a witches' coven, then you should not leave your child unsupervised in front of a computer screen.

There is software that you can install on the computer that will enable you to track everything your child has seen on the computer. Some parents may say, "But isn't that spying on my kids?" Of course it is! You are the parent. You are *supposed* to know what your kids are doing. You are responsible for their welfare. You should know exactly what your children are reading and posting on MySpace and Facebook. You should know if they are visiting chat rooms, being exposed to—or engaging in—sexual talk, or viewing obscene images. If you paid for the computer, the Internet connection, and the house your kids live in, you have a right and a responsibility to "spy" on your kids.

A Matter of Life and Death

Paul writes in 1 Corinthians 15:33, "Do not be misled: 'Bad company corrupts good character.'" You have a responsibility to know who your kids' friends are. Your children's peers have an enormous influence on their values, worldview, and behavior—and sometimes even a tragic influence.

David and Kara both came from Christian homes in Lancaster County, Pennsylvania. He was eighteen; she was fourteen. Against their parents' wishes, they began dating each other.

Kara had a page on MySpace. It featured her photo—the playful, innocent image of a blond, brown-eyed teen, mugging for the camera with her lips clamped shut to hide her braces. The page was girlishly adorned with rainbow stripes and pink-edged boxes which displayed her interests:

> JESUS!! church, my youth group, other youth groups, family, friends, my doggie, KIDS, babysitting, soccer, basketball, football, talking on the phone, food, eating, taking pictures, cooking, guitar, the beach, camp, taking walks, riding my bike, just being outside, having parties, OH YEAH BABY, going to parties, making new friends, helping out, music, CANDY, PUSH-POPS, shopping, hugging.

In other words, she was an average Christian teenager with many perfectly wholesome interests. But her life was about to take a sudden, deadly turn.

One night in November 2005, Kara told her mom she was planning to spend the night at her girlfriend's house. It was a lie. She spent that night with David.

Early the next morning, David drove Kara back to her house in his car. Kara's parents were waiting for them, having learned of Kara's deception from one of her friends. Kara's father told her to go into the house so that he could talk to David—but he didn't know what David had tucked into the duffel bag in his hand.

While Kara stood and watched, saying nothing, David dropped the duffel bag on the lawn in front of the house. He pulled out a pair of guns and, with cold-blooded deliberation, shot Kara's father in the head. As Kara's father lay bleeding in the front yard, David stormed into the house, located Kara's mother and shot her—killing her in front of Kara's two siblings, ages eleven and fifteen.

David ran outside and dashed to his car—and Kara ran to join him. Together they fled the crime scene. Within hours, the two missing teens were the subject of an intense multi-state manhunt.

The following day, in a rural section of central Indiana, police caught up with David and Kara after he crashed his car into a tree. In addition to murder and other charges, David was initially charged with kidnapping. That charge was later dropped when Kara admitted that she went willingly with the young killer. The fourteen-year-old girl intended to marry the young man who had murdered her parents.

David is now serving two consecutive life sentences without the possibility of parole. Kara was placed in foster care.[12]

Who are your kids hanging out with, calling and texting, spending time online with? Who are your kids emotionally involved with? Who are their peers? How are they being influenced? The answers to those questions could be a matter of life and death.

Never give up on your kids. Pray *with* your children—and pray *for* them. Pray that they hold on to the faith you have taught them throughout their childhood. The teen years are filled with craziness, but God's truth will restore sanity to your family. Even as the crosses are disappearing from the world around you, keep the cross at the center of your family life.

Read God's Word together. Take time to sit down with your kids, look them in the eye, listen to their problems, take delight in their interests, and talk to them. When your children reach those turbulent teenage years, persevere with them and love them through it. You may think they aren't listening, and that you have lost your influence with them, but that's when they are watching you most closely!

They are testing their limits—but they are also testing *you* and watching you to see how you will respond. They will argue with everything you say and call you "old-fashioned" and "clueless"—but they will remember what you say. They will ponder it and consider it—and some of it may just get through.

Chapter Seven

Restoring Sanity in the Church

In February 2008, the Archbishop of Canterbury, Rowan Williams, told a BBC radio interviewer that the United Kingdom needs to "face up to the fact that some of its citizens"—that is, British Muslims—"do not relate to the British legal system." Therefore, the British legal system needed to, at some point, adopt parts of Islamic Sharia law—a legal code based on the Quran, the sayings of Mohammed, and centuries of tradition.

The Archbishop seemed to be saying that maintaining two unequal sets of laws was somehow fairer than equal justice under the law. He said, "An approach to law which simply said, 'There is one law for everybody and that is all there is to be said'—I think that's a bit of a danger."

But what is "dangerous" about *equality*? What is fair about having unequal legal standards for different citizens in the same society? What about the danger to British Muslim women if they lose the protection of British law and suddenly became vulnerable to the harsh penalties of Sharia law?[1]

Dr. Williams' thinking on this issue seems to be based on feelings. He witnesses the looming social crisis caused by the great influx of Muslims into British society. He wants to demonstrate sensitivity to the feelings of the Islamic community—so he loses sight of centuries-old principles of equal justice. Christendom and western civilization desperately need wise, thoughtful, principled *leadership*—but the Archbishop of Canterbury offers only feelings and compromise.

Even many Islamic Britons were appalled at the Archbishop's words. Baroness Sayeeda Hussain Warsi, a Conservative Party member of Britain's "Shadow Cabinet" and a Sunni Muslim, issued a stinging rebuke to the Archbishop: "We must ensure that people of all backgrounds and religions are treated equally before the law. Freedom under the law allows respect for some religious practices. But let's be clear: All British citizens must be subject to British laws developed through parliament and the courts."[2]

In the United States, evangelical leader Charles Colson responded, "In real-world Muslim communities throughout Europe, coercion is so commonplace that duly-constituted governments there no longer wield justice among its citizens. The imams do. And where would the Archbishop draw the line? At husbands beating their wives for wearing Western clothes or maybe stoning a woman accused of adultery?" Colson went on to cite the observations of my friend, Bishop Michael Nazir-Ali:

> Williams's fellow bishop, Michael Nazir-Ali, recently spoke about what he calls "no-go zones" in Muslim communities where Christians dare not enter. As a result of death threats, Bishop Nazir-Ali and his family require police protection.
>
> Nazir-Ali, whose father had to leave Pakistan after converting to Christianity, told the *UK Telegraph* that Sharia is "in tension" with "fundamental aspects" of Anglo-American law. That is because our "legal tradition" is "rooted in the quite different moral and spiritual vision deriving from the Bible." This crucial difference seems to have escaped the Archbishop of Canterbury.

The Archbishop is raising the white flag of surrender to the global advance of Islam while implicitly admitting that the Christian church is dying, its influence fading. As Colson concludes, "There are an estimated 1.6 million Muslims in Great Britain. By some estimates, more people attend mosque than go to Anglican churches every week. Judging by recent comments by the Archbishop of Canterbury, it is easy to see why... This weakness is the stuff that empty churches are made of."[3]

Just seven months after the Archbishop's pronouncement, his prediction came to pass. On September 14, 2008, *The Sunday Times* of London published a news story under the shocking headline: "Revealed: UK's First Official Sharia Courts." The story announced:

Islamic law has been officially adopted in Britain, with Sharia courts given powers to rule on Muslim civil cases.

The government has quietly sanctioned the powers for Sharia judges to rule on cases ranging from divorce and financial disputes to those involving domestic violence.

Rulings issued by a network of five Sharia courts are enforceable with the full power of the judicial system, through the county courts or High Court....

It has now emerged that Sharia courts with these powers have been set up in London, Birmingham, Bradford and Manchester with the network's headquarters in Nuneaton, Warwickshire. Two more courts are being planned for Glasgow and Edinburgh.[4]

Columnist A. Millar, writing in the "This Sceptered Isle" column for *The Brussels Journal*, made this ominous observation:

A couple of years ago even, it seemed unimaginable that Britain would adopt Islamic law.

We have sunk further and quicker than we thought possible. Today we learned that Sharia courts (which have operated illegally in Britain until now) are being re-classed as tribunal hearings, making their judgments legally binding....

The Sharia courts operating in Britain will hear and pass legally binding judgment on cases involving divorce, financial disputes, and even domestic violence. But, it will not end there. According to the *Daily Mail*, Sharia court officials have said that they hope... to establish Sharia law for everyone in Britain. Only yesterday, the *Sun* newspaper showed a video of radical clerics announcing plans to take over Britain. [One of them said:] "It may be by pure conversion that Britain will become an Islamic state. We may never need to conquer it from the outside."

This, among other similar pronouncements, was made at a rally billed as a debate on whether the West had "learned the lessons" of the September 11 terrorist attacks. Apparently, we have not.[5]

You might ask, "Could Sharia law ever come to American courtrooms?" The answer: It already has.

In 2009, a divorced woman went to a New Jersey family court seeking a restraining order against her Moroccan ex-husband. He would repeatedly come to her home and force her to have sex with him. She struggled, she wept—but he insisted that Islamic law gave him the right to do anything he wanted with her. Judge Joseph Charles put the man's imam on the stand and asked him questions about Islamic law. Then he delivered his decision—and denied the woman's request for a restraining order.

If any other non-Muslim ex-husband had been accused of such acts, a restraining order would have been granted almost automatically—and the man would likely have been charged with rape. But the court sided with an Islamic ex-husband and Islamic law, while refusing to apply the laws of the United States of America. Robert Spencer, director of JihadWatch.com, said that the judge's decision was "strictly in line with Islamic law, which does indeed declare that a wife may not refuse her husband sex under virtually any circumstances. The only legal framework that would not consider marital rape to be sexual assault is Sharia."

It took the woman more than a year to get Judge Charles' decision overturned on appeal. During that time, she lived in fear, without the protection of the American legal system.[6]

The Scriptures tell us that we are to be kind, compassionate, and loving toward immigrants. "Do not mistreat an alien or oppress him," says the Lord, "for you were aliens in Egypt" (Exodus 22:21). That should be our guiding principle in our dealings with all immigrants, including those of the Islamic faith. But this does not mean that we should bend our laws to accommodate Sharia law, nor should we ignore the fact that Islamic extremists are determined to turn the entire world into an Islamic state.

One day, we will look back and ask ourselves, "Why did we timidly surrender instead of standing our ground? Why were we so cowardly and foolish as to allow militant Islamists to take away our freedom and our way of life without even a whimper of protest?"

When the crosses are gone, we will have no one but ourselves to blame.

A Dead Corpse of Religion

Throughout the Bible, God warns against yielding to emotion instead of obeying His truth. After He led Israel out of Egypt and into the wilderness, He listened to the grumbling of the people. He knew that if the Israelites trusted their emotions, their resentful feelings would lead them into idolatry. Driven by lust, they would exchange God's truth for demonic gods connected to the cycles of nature, sexual promiscuity, and human sacrifices.

So God told His people to obey rational principles and keep His law. He answered the emotion of hate with the words, "You shall not murder." He answered the emotion of lust with, "You shall not commit adultery." He answered the emotion of greed with, "You shall not steal." He answered the emotion of envy with, "You shall not covet." He answered the emotion of bitterness with, "You shall not give false testimony."

When Israel obeyed God's law, the people were blessed. When Israel followed feelings and lusts, the people suffered the awful consequences. This biblical principle is still in force today.

God calls the Christian church to believe the Bible, God's Word, which has stood the test of time. Faith, after all, is not just giving mental assent to a set of doctrines and creeds. Faith is a total commitment to trust and obey God. It's a decision to live our lives according to His promises. Faith does not mean we will never experience feelings of doubt or questioning. But a person of faith holds on to a commitment to trust and obey God, confident that one day all of the doubts and questions will be answered.

God has given us more than enough reason to believe His Word and place our trust in His Son. The rational evidence for faith is strong and sound. Most of the struggles we experience in our faith occur not in the realm of reason and evidence, but in the realm of our emotions. In *Mere Christianity*, C. S. Lewis explains:

> I am not asking anyone to accept Christianity if his best reasoning tells him that the weight of evidence is against it. That is not the point at which faith comes in. But supposing a man's reason once decides that the weight of the evidence is for it. I can tell that man what is going to happen to him in the next few weeks. There will come a moment when there is bad news, or he is in trouble, or is living among a lot of other people who do not believe it, and all at once his emotions will rise up and carry out a sort of blitz on his belief.... I am not talking of moments at which any real new reasons against Christianity turn up. Those have to be faced and that is a different matter. I am talking about moments where a mere mood rises up against it.
>
> Now faith, in the sense in which I am here using the word, is the art of holding onto things your reason has once accepted, in spite of your changing moods. For moods will change, whatever view your reason takes. I know that by experience.[7]

That is why faith must be a commitment to God's truth—a commitment to persevering through times of changing emotions and shifting moods. Let us give God no superficial commitment, but cast ourselves on Him in complete trust.

I am not denying the importance of emotions in the worship of God. But any brand of Christianity that offers nothing more than an ecstatic emotional experience or a faith without evidence is at odds with biblical truth. The faith of the Bible is one in which God approaches us, saying: "Come now, let us reason together.... Though your sins are like scarlet, they shall be as white as snow; though they are red as crimson, they shall be like wool" (Isaiah 1:18).

The faith of the Bible is a faith in which every believer is called upon to have sound reasons for believing, rooted in absolute truth under the Lordship of Jesus Christ. As the apostle Peter tells us, "But in your hearts set apart Christ as Lord. Always be prepared to give an answer to everyone who asks you to give the reason for the hope that you have. But do this with gentleness and respect" (1 Peter 3:15).

Ours is a reasonable faith, supported by a mountain of philosophical, historical, and yes, scientific evidence.[8] However, the true measure of our faith is how we put those beliefs into practice. Faith must take control of our will. Paul tells us in Romans 1:5 that God calls us not to an emotional experience, but "to the obedience that comes from faith."

A Fortress Mentality

The spiritual roots of America go down deep into Protestant theology, intertwined with Puritan thought. This rich spiritual heritage has influenced the very Constitution we revere and the Federalist papers which outline our form of government. Anyone who denies the rich Christian influence in the thinking of our Founding Fathers is espousing revisionist history.

The Puritans were a highly literate people who valued education and intellectual pursuits. They built schools and colleges that offered a rigorous classical education combined with religious learning. A student who graduated from a Puritan school had a strong foundation in philosophy, science, the humanities, and the Word of God.

Puritan leader John Winthrop envisioned the Puritan community of New England as "a city upon a hill"—a shining example to the rest of the world. In 1636, just six years after settling in the New World, the Puritans founded Harvard College. One of the distinguished graduates of that college, Puritan minister Cotton Mather, stated that "ignorance is the mother not of devotion but Heresy."[9]

By the nineteenth century, Puritan influence was waning in America, and the influence of the Age of Reason was growing. Rationalist philosophers such as David Hume (1711–1776) and Immanuel Kant (1724–1804) claimed that the only truth is that which is demonstrated by the five senses. In their view, faith in God did not meet that test.

By the early 1800s, this naturalistic view had spawned a European theological movement called "higher criticism." Centered in Germany, this movement spread across Europe. The higher critics prided themselves on a "rational" and "scientific" approach to biblical criticism. In reality, their approach was nothing of the kind. Dyson Hague (1857-1935), an Anglican evangelical theologian, observed that the higher critics' theories were founded "upon their own subjective conclusions. They have based their conclusions largely upon the very dubious basis of the [Scripture writer's] style and supposed literary qualifications."[10]

In other words, the higher critics started with a bias. They assumed that every Bible story involving God's miraculous intervention—the Flood, the exodus from Egypt, the fall of Jericho, the resurrection of Jesus—must be a fable. Their assumptions determined their conclusions.

It didn't take long for the ideas of the higher critics to jump the Atlantic and infect the universities, seminaries, and churches in America. Mainline denominations embraced the higher critical views. Soon, from pulpits across America, the word went out that the Bible is nothing more than a collection of inspirational fables, stitched together by anonymous editors. It is alright to admire the Bible for its poetry and stories, but it should not be taken seriously as the living Word of God.

In her book *Total Truth*, Christian scholar Nancy Pearcey described the American evangelical backlash against the higher critics' views:

A "religion of the heart" was not enough to respond to the intellectual challenges emerging in the nineteenth century, especially Darwinism and higher criticism. Later evangelists like Dwight L. Moody and Billy Sunday tried to counter the new ideas with sheer revivalist fervor. The fervor, however, began to take on a brittle, defensive edge. And the more Christians sought to prop up their faith with mere emotional intensity, the more it appeared to be an irrational belief....

Unable to answer the great intellectual questions of the day, many conservative Christians turned their back on mainstream culture and developed a fortress mentality.... "The intellectual foundations of Judeo-Christian theism were being questioned as never before," writes historian Joel Carpenter. "Fundamentalist leaders were caught unprepared to respond to the critiques of scientific naturalism, whether applied to natural history [Darwinism] or to the study of the Bible [higher criticism]...."

Today evangelicalism is still emerging from the fundamentalist era.[11]

Nineteenth century evangelicals and fundamentalists reacted against higher criticism with an emotionalism of their own. They largely withdrew from the world, abandoning the universities and the mainstream culture, allowing society to become divided into secular and Christian camps.

As the evangelical church withdrew, Darwin's theory of evolution advanced on the scene, supplying atheists and agnostics with a cover of scientific respectability. The church, instead of developing intellectual arguments to refute the speculations of the higher critics and the Darwinists, hid within a snail-shell of anti-intellectualism. The theologically liberal mainline denominations saw the anti-intellectualism of evangelicals as proof of ignorance and backward thinking. The split between mainline Christianity and evangelicalism continues to this day.

It was a mistake for evangelicals to withdraw into a fortress mentality while surrendering the culture to secularism. As Mark Steyn observes in *America Alone*, the lack of Christian influence in our culture makes society vulnerable to infiltration and attack:

[Mainline denominations] are sinking beneath the bog of their own relativist mush, while Islam is the West's fastest-growing religion. There's no market for a faith that has no faith in itself.

One reason why the developed world has a difficult job grappling with the Islamist threat is that it doesn't take religion seriously. It condescends to it....

If ever there were a time for a strong voice from the heart of Christianity, this would be it.[12]

If Christianity is to speak with a strong voice, it must maintain a strong faith, based on enduring principles that come from God's Word.

An Enigma—and a Stigma

You may recall that immediately following the 9/11 attacks in 2001, church attendance in America soared. People who had not seen the inside of a church in years suddenly felt a desperate need for God. But as life returned to normal, church attendance fell.

According to a poll by the Pew Forum on Religion and Public Life, there is one religion that received a sustained, long-term benefit from the post-9/11 religious surge: Islam. "Fifty-four percent of Americans hold a favorable impression of Islam," Charles Colson wrote in early 2002, "'significantly' higher than at this time a year ago."[13] This is truly amazing when you realize that the 9/11 attacks were carried out in the name of Islam.

The 2002 Pew poll also showed that nearly half of all evangelicals who call themselves "highly committed" agree with the statement, "Many religions can lead to eternal life." It's as if nearly half of the "highly committed" Christians in the evangelical church reject the Lord's own words in John 14:6: "I am the way and the truth and the life. No one comes to the Father except through me." This, too, is an astounding finding.

A repeat of that poll, conducted five years later, showed that the number of evangelicals who believe that many religions lead to eternal life seems to be climbing. In June 2008, *Time* magazine reported:

> The Pew Forum on Religion and Public Life last year surveyed 35,000 Americans, and found that 70 percent of respondents agreed with the statement, "Many religions can lead to eternal life." Even more remarkable was the fact that 57 percent of Evangelical Christians were willing to accept that theirs might not be the only path to salvation, since most Christians historically have embraced the words of Jesus, in the Gospel of John, that "no one comes to the Father except through me." Even as mainline churches had become

more tolerant, the exclusivity of Christianity's path to heaven has long been one of the Evangelicals' fundamental tenets. The new poll suggests a major shift, at least in the pews.[14]

As Charles Colson concludes, there is a growing mindset in the church that says, "The important thing about a religion is how it makes us feel, not whether it's true. In fact, questions about truth claims are considered impolite, uncivil, and even intolerant. If a particular belief makes a person happy, who are we to judge?... Christians need to help people understand that religion is not a matter of sentiment. It is a matter of truth."[15]

Perhaps these findings also explain why increasing numbers of evangelical Christians and evangelical churches are surrendering the cross—deliberately removing the cross in order to avoid "offending" anyone. In North Carolina in 2004, the Caldwell Memorial Presbyterian Church saw its membership— and income—declining. To make up the budget shortfall, the church decided to lease its buildings to an Islamic school. The Islamic group demanded that the church remove all of its crosses. The church agreed, took down the crosses, and turned its facilities over for the indoctrination of young souls in the tenets of Islam.[16]

Of course, many so-called "seeker-friendly" churches have removed the cross to avoid offending the "seekers" they want to draw into their churches. One such church is Christ Community Church in Spring Lake, Minnesota, now known as C3Exchange. The decision to remove the towering cross from the front of the building—and remove "Christ" from the name of the church— was explained by Pastor Ian Lawton: "Our community has been a really open-minded community for some years now. We've had a number of Muslim people, Jewish people, Buddhists, atheists.... Our community is a place where people can come to exchange ideas."

In a sermon, Lawton once called the crucifixion of Christ "cosmic child abuse." He adds, "The cross has become a negative symbol for a lot of people." He plans to replace the missing cross with symbols of a globe, a heart, and the word "Exchange"—symbols which, he says, express "one love" for "all people."[17]

How tragic! Hasn't he ever heard that the cross of Christ is the greatest expression in history of one love for all people?

Perhaps the cross is disappearing from our churches because there is a lack of coherent understanding about what the cross means. In our churches today, there is very little preaching on the cross. There are very few faithful voices that still preach the cross of Christ.

As the pulpit goes, so goes the pew. As the pew goes, so goes the nation.

I have heard and read of pastors who have spoken of the cross of Christ in the most outrageous terms. They have called it "a turn-off for unbelievers," "an unnecessary symbol for churches," "old and archaic," and "a hindrance to reaching out to the unchurched."

For many pastors, the cross of Christ has become an enigma—and a stigma.

During his days on earth, Jesus told his disciples, "If anyone would come after me, he must deny himself and take up his cross and follow me" (Mark 8:34). The early Christians counted it a privilege to carry their Lord's cross. All too many Christians today are ashamed of that cross.

The Shadow and the Reality

The early Christians chose the cross as the symbol of the Christian faith. They could have chosen the manger scene depicting the place where the baby Jesus was born. They could have chosen the carpenter's bench where Jesus worked in Nazareth. They could have chosen the boat from which Jesus taught the crowd in Galilee. They could have chosen the towel Jesus wore around his waist when He washed the disciples' feet. They could have chosen the stone which was rolled away from the grave at His mighty Resurrection. They could have chosen a throne to depict His sovereign reign as King of Kings and Lord of Lords. They could have chosen a dove to symbolize the Holy Spirit who testified to Jesus at the time of His baptism.

But the early Christians didn't choose any of those symbols. Instead they chose the symbol of the cross.

I think it is significant that the early Christians did not choose the crucifix, the image of Jesus nailed to the cross. The early Christians chose an empty cross. The image of the crucifix was unknown until the 6th century AD.

I believe the early Christians deliberately chose the empty cross because they wanted to emphasize the empty cross and the empty tomb.

With the empty cross, God declared that the wages of sin were paid in full. Redemption was complete. The perfect sacrifice had been offered. The defeat of Satan was accomplished. The mystery of what comes after death was solved. The plan of God was revealed. On the cross, God did not just *find* a solution for sin. He *became* the solution.

The human race glimpsed a foreshadowing of the cross in the first book of the Bible—Genesis. There, Adam and Eve sinned—and God shed the blood of an innocent lamb and covered their nakedness with its skin. This was an object lesson, teaching the first human beings that, to atone for sin, innocent blood must be shed. Adam and Eve didn't understand the meaning of the slain lamb, because it was a *shadow* of the cross, not the cross itself.

In the book of Exodus, God told Moses to kill a lamb and sprinkle the blood on the door-posts of Hebrew homes. When the angel of the Lord saw the blood on the door-posts, he passed them by and everyone inside that home was spared. The Hebrew people couldn't fully understand the meaning of the blood on the door-posts because that blood was only a *shadow* of the bloodstained cross, not the cross itself.

Down through the pages of the Old Testament, God lifted up the cross so that its shadow became larger and more distinct. A thousand years before Christ, King David wrote Psalm 22 under the inspiration of the Holy Spirit. There, he described in precise detail exactly what it feels like to be crucified. And 700 years before the cross, the prophet Isaiah looked forward with the eyes of faith and described how God Himself would pay the penalty for our disobedience: "But he was pierced for our transgressions, he was crushed for our iniquities; the punishment that brought us peace was upon him, and by his wounds we are healed" (Isaiah 53:5).

Centuries came and went. Jesus was born and lived among us. Finally, He was crucified. The long foreshadowing of the cross had fulfilled its purpose. It had heightened expectations, while proclaiming the coming reality of the cross. On that Good Friday, the shadow gave way to reality.

The Bible teaches that, in order for God's justice to prevail, sin must be punished. For God's justice to prevail, the problem of human sin and rebellion must be cured. And because the only permanent cure for sin is the shedding of innocent blood, *God had to shed His own blood*—the most innocent blood of all.

The animal sacrifices of the Old Testament provided only a temporary cover for sin. The cross of Christ solved the sin problem forever. The animal sacrifices reminded God's people of the terrible cost of sin. The cross of Christ paid that cost in full. Animal sacrifices foreshadowed the cross. The cross itself was the reality.

The Hated and Rejected Cross

Many Christians today have lost sight of the meaning of the cross. That is why they no longer preach the cross and why they are so willing to remove it from the church.

The Christian doctrine of atonement states that when Jesus was crucified, He took the punishment for our sins upon Himself to satisfy the demands of God's justice so that God could forgive our sins. Yet a British church leader has written a book, published by an evangelical publisher, which *denies* the doctrine of atonement. This man says that the doctrine of atonement is tantamount to "child abuse—a vengeful Father punishing his Son for an offence he has not even committed."[18] Has this man never read God's Word? The crucifixion was an act of love toward humanity, not vengeance, not "child abuse."

The further we move away from the cross and its meaning, the deeper into darkness we descend. As this church leader and his colleagues reject the cross, the evangelical church in England is in full retreat. Meanwhile, Sharia law is burrowing its way into the British legal system. All across England and Europe, churches are emptying out and becoming museums while some of the largest mosques in the world, seating upwards of 70,000 people, are being erected.

Increasingly, throughout the Western world, the cross is hated and rejected. Churches used to raise the cross high as a beacon to the lost. Now many churches hide the cross so they will not scare anyone away. These churches are hastening our culture's departure from the truth.

Whenever human beings elevate their own wisdom above God's, the wisdom of God becomes foolishness to them. Whenever human beings think they can save themselves, the idea of God coming in human form, dying on a cross, and paying the price for their sin becomes foolishness to them. We are seeing exactly what the Apostle Paul told us would happen: "For the message of the cross is foolishness to those who are perishing, but to us who are being saved it is the power of God" (1 Corinthians 1:18). In the original language, the Greek word for "foolishness" is "mōria" (μωρία), from which we get the English word "moron."

Paul is saying that, to the unbeliever, it is moronic to think that a man who died on a cross 2,000 years ago can grant anyone eternal life. It is moronic to think that the shed-blood of the Man-God Jesus Christ can purchase forgiveness and eternal redemption for human beings. To the people of this world, the cross is moronic, it is an offense, it is foolishness.

That is why the cross was removed from Caldwell Memorial Presbyterian Church and Christ Community Church. That is why employers try to remove the cross from around the necks of employees, why school administrators try to remove the cross from the necks of their students, why the College of William and Mary removed the cross from the altar of Wren Chapel, why the Communists removed the crosses from churches across Russia and Eastern Europe, and it is why the ACLU tries to remove the cross from every public place in America.

The cross is foolishness and an offense to Muslims. Islam teaches that Jesus was a prophet, but it denies that Jesus was crucified. Six centuries after Christ, when Muhammad is said to have dictated the Quran, it was written that those who tried to crucify Jesus "did not kill him nor did they crucify him, but it appeared to them so...." (Quran, Surah 4, verse 157)[19] Islamic tradition teaches that Allah whisked Jesus up to heaven and the evildoers were fooled into crucifying Judas Iscariot in His place. Muslims could not accept the fact that God would allow a sinless man to die for the sins of others.

The truth of the cross was, to them, foolishness and offensive.

The message of the cross is, "You need a Savior," and that is a profoundly offensive message among those who insist that they are the masters of their own fate—the humanists, the secularists, the atheists, the agnostics, the Darwinists, the apostates. The cross is a message of love to humankind—but to those who would rather perish than accept God's love, it is an offensive message. They want no part of it.

The cross cannot be neutral. It will either bring you peace or make you angry. It will either save you eternally or judge you eternally. The cross will either reconcile you to God or bear witness against you in the Day of Judgment. It will either cleanse you of sin or remind you of your rebellion against God.

The cross disturbs the psyche. It troubles the soul. It forces you to make a decision: Will you say yes to Jesus Christ—or no? Are you with Him—or against Him? The cross leaves no room for neutrality, and that is why so many people want to remove the cross from our world.

"It Is Finished"

In Jesus' day, whenever a debt was settled—either paid in full or forgiven—the creditor would take the canceled promissory note to the home of the debtor and nail it to the wooden lintel over the door. In this way, any passerby could see that the debt was canceled.

That is what the cross is all about. Our debt was nailed to the cross—an announcement to the world that the debt has been fully paid. That is the imagery Paul uses when he writes to the Colossians that Jesus has forgiven our debts, "having canceled out the certificate of debt consisting of decrees against us, which was hostile to us; and He has taken it out of the way, having nailed it to the cross" (Colossians 2:13).

Whenever you feel guilt or shame over the sins of the past, simply say, "Jesus nailed it all to the cross." Whenever Satan accuses you of failure, say, "Jesus nailed it all to the cross." If anyone tries to manipulate you with guilt, say, "Jesus nailed it all to the cross." Whenever you begin to doubt your own salvation, say, "Jesus nailed it all to the Cross."

When Jesus hung on the cross, the last word he spoke before he died was, "Tetelestai!" In English, this means, "It is finished!" In the original Greek, Jesus spoke this word in the perfect tense, which means, "It is finished *now*, and it will *forever* remain finished." It was the Lord's proclamation that He had accomplished all that He had come to earth to do. Of His own free will, He had endured the punishment of sin in our place.

When He said, "It is finished," the curtain of the great temple in Jerusalem was torn from top to bottom. That curtain symbolized the separation of God from humanity—and when the curtain was torn asunder, our alienation from God was ended. We could approach Him directly through Jesus Christ.

The cross of Christ gave power to the powerless. It gave strength to the weak. It brought salvation to repentant sinners. It brought hope to the hopeless. It gave peace to troubled hearts.

What was true then it is still true today.

Having served as an evangelical Episcopal priest in the United States, I have often been viewed as an oddity within my own former denomination. I have even been ridiculed for my orthodox faith by former colleagues. A bishop (who passed away a few years ago) once said to me, "How can you have earned a Ph.D. from a highly respectable university—yet you still believe in the authenticity of the Gospels' account?"

I explained my views in favor of the historical virgin birth, the Lord's miracles, and His resurrection. I mentioned that the Apostle Paul wrote to the Christians in Corinth and cited tangible evidence of the resurrection, reminding them that the risen Lord had "appeared to more than five hundred of the brothers at the same time, most of whom are still living" (1 Corinthians 15:6). These eyewitness accounts were well known in the early church—yet liberal scholars, 2,000 years later, chose to dismiss those accounts on the assumption that miracles cannot happen.

I pointed out that most of the non-archaeological evidence for the destruction of Pompeii is a single eyewitness account by a teenager, Pliny the Younger. How can we accept Pliny's account as historically accurate while choosing to dismiss the word of 500 eyewitnesses?

After hearing my arguments, the bishop said, "I had never considered such views before."

One of the great tragedies of American evangelical history is that we evangelicals surrendered to secularism and liberalism without a struggle. When asked, "What is your evidence?," we replied, "We don't need evidence. We accept it by faith." We offered nothing but sheer belief, unsupported by evidence.

The writers of the New Testament would have been shocked to hear the Gospel proclaimed in this way. When Peter preached in Jerusalem on Pentecost in Acts 2, he offered evidence upon evidence for the resurrection. When Paul preached in Athens in Acts 17, he debated with the pagans and secularists, offering rational arguments for the Gospel.

The early Christian apostles and evangelists were hardly anti-intellectuals. They did not say, "You don't need evidence. Just accept it on faith." Theirs was an intellectually robust message aimed not only at the emotions, but also at the intellect of their audiences.

R. C. Sproul, founder of Ligonier Ministries, says we need passion and intellect, emotion and reason. "We live in what may be the most anti-intellectual period in the history of Western civilization," he writes. "We must have passion—indeed hearts on fire for the things of God. But that passion must resist with intensity the anti-intellectual spirit of the world."[20]

Os Guinness underscores the tragedy of anti-intellectualism in the church: "Anti-intellectualism is a disposition to discount the importance of truth and the life of the mind.... At root, evangelical anti-intellectualism is both a scandal and a sin. It is a scandal in the sense of being an offense and a stumbling block that needlessly hinders serious people from considering the Christian faith and coming to Christ. It is a sin because it is a refusal, contrary to Jesus' two great commandments, to love the Lord our God with our minds."[21]

A Challenge to the Church

Somewhere along the way, we evangelicals have lost our intellectual edge. It is not because evangelicals are stupid—though many are intellectually lazy. Rather, I blame decades of evangelical anti-intellectualism in the pulpit, and the pastors who have preached, "accept it on faith," instead of training Christians to "be prepared to give an answer to everyone who asks" (1 Peter 3:15). If we offer no evidence for faith, then the people around us have no more reason to believe our Gospel than they have to believe the Jehovah's Witnesses or Eastern religion or Scientology or atheism.

I am not saying that the Gospel is only for intellectuals. Far from it. Millions have come to Christ in simple, trusting faith. They didn't demand evidence. They were drawn by the Holy Spirit to a childlike faith, and the Gospel is so simple a child can receive it. But there are many people who have doubts and questions—and that is why God tells us to always "be prepared to give an answer" that is rooted in God's truth.

When anti-intellectualism is brought to full term, it gives birth to all sorts of false belief systems and false teachers who spring up within the church and lead many astray. When feelings have dethroned the Christian intellect, the result is an anemic and emaciated church—much like the church we have today:

- A church which emphasizes only a "what's-in-it-for-me" spirituality.
- A church which has no impact on the secular society.
- A church of mushy-thinking, pew-warming spectators who have no interest in serving or evangelizing their neighbors.
- A church in which the Gospel of Jesus Christ competes with dozens of false, seductive "spin-off" Gospels—the prosperity Gospel, the social Gospel, the "me" Gospel, the liberation Gospel, the universalism Gospel, the New Age Gospel, and so forth.

God has not called us to be intellectually lazy. He has called us to be a community of disciples who feel deeply, care deeply, and think deeply about the things of God. He demands everything of us, including our intellect: "Love the Lord your God with all your heart and with all your soul and with all your strength *and with all your mind*" (Luke 10:27).

Jesus said that we are the light of the world and the salt of the earth. By reflecting God's truth and the knowledge of His Word, we illuminate the world. As salt seasons and preserves food, so we season and preserve society. If the culture around us sinks into darkness and corruption, it is because we have failed to be salt and light. When the crosses are gone, we will have no one to blame but ourselves.

So I'm issuing a plea:

- It's time for pastors to stop giving "feel-good" motivational talks and get back to teaching God's truth.
- It's time for pastors to openly renounce the desire to merely fill pews and collection plates.
- It's time to preach *all* of God's Word, the parts that comfort us, the parts that challenge us, and the parts that call us to repentance.
- It's time to proclaim "thus says the Lord," even if it means that the crowd thins out.
- It's time all of us, both clergy and laypeople, to return to a bold, confident, intellectually-robust declaration of the Gospel of Jesus Christ.

If we wish to reach the hearts and minds of the people around us, we must restore sanity to the church—a sanity which is found only in the Word of God. As we return the church to the Word of God, let's begin once more to plant the cross of Christ in the ground of this hostile—and hurting—world.

Chapter Eight

Agents of Sanity in a World Gone Mad

On September 17, 2005, Mahmoud Ahmadinejad, the President of Iran, stood before the General Assembly of the United Nations and said, "From the beginning of time, humanity has longed for the day when justice, peace, equality and compassion envelop the world. All of us can contribute to the establishment of such a world. When that day comes, the ultimate promise of all divine religions will be fulfilled with the emergence of a perfect human being who is heir to all prophets and pious men. He will lead the world to justice and absolute peace."[1]

Who is the "perfect human being" Ahmadinejad prayed for? In Shiite eschatology, he is called the "Mahdi," the Divinely Guided One. The Mahdi is a warrior-messiah, also known as the Twelfth Imam, who has been hidden from the world by Allah since AD 941. According to Shiite belief, the Mahdi will return after a time of chaos and apocalyptic war that will leave millions dead. When the Mahdi appears as the savior of humanity, he will bring peace and justice to the world and rid humanity of religious error. The Mahdi will reign on earth for several years, and then bring forth a day of judgment and the end of the world.[2]

When you study the life of Mahmoud Ahmadinejad, one thing becomes clear: He thinks *he* is the long-prophesied Mahdi. After his 2005 UN address, he claimed that—as he spoke to the UN delegates for nearly half an hour—he was bathed in a green aura of heavenly light. He said that all of the world leaders who heard him speak were transfixed by the light, and did not move or even blink throughout his speech.[3]

In addition to calling for the destruction of Israel, Ahmadinejad has said that the world is already engaged in a war "between the World of Arrogance (the Christian West) and the Islamic world," and he claims that "a world without America and Zionism" is "attainable."[4]

Now imagine this man—the self-styled Mahdi of Shiite prophecy—with nuclear weapons under his control. Is he afraid of nuclear war? Absolutely not! Nuclear holocaust is his heart's fondest wish. He believes that touching off a global nuclear war would fulfill prophecy and reveal him to the world.

So I ask you: How do you deter a nuclear-armed zealot who can't wait to launch Armageddon? Answer: You can't. That is the threat the world faces from militant Islam. This man's ideology is a menace to all of humanity.

My friend, we are living in a world gone mad. Now the question is: Can this world be restored to sanity?

Is there *any* hope?

I believe there is. That hope lies with people like you and me, people who are willing to be agents of sanity in a dangerous world. The Lord Himself has called us to be "salt and light" in a corrupt and dark world. He has called us to boldly proclaim His truth in a world full of deception.

We must accept the challenge of our times. We must offer God's hope to a world that is beyond all hope.

A World Shaped by Faith

In every time in history, it is largely the religion of a culture that impacts and shapes that culture. Have you ever wondered why, for so many centuries, Western civilization led the world in scientific advancement and technology? Quite simply, it is because of the Christian worldview. The great scientists of past ages were committed believers. They were convinced that a rational God had created an orderly universe, so they searched for the laws by which God had constructed the universe—and they *found* those laws.

To Johannes Kepler, God was the Great Mathematician—and that is why Kepler discovered the laws of planetary motion that bear his name. To Sir Isaac Newton, God was the Great Engineer—and faith drove him to derive the laws of gravitation and motion, laying the groundwork for classical mechanics and engineering. To Michael Faraday, God was the Great Physicist—and his supreme confidence in the orderliness of God's creation led him to astonishing discoveries in the fields of electricity, electromagnetism, and electrochemistry.

The Christian faith has stirred great social movements in society. The end of the slave trade in England was brought about by the efforts of William Wilberforce and others whose Christian faith filled them with compassion for oppressed people—and outrage against injustice. In America, the abolition movement was led by the Quakers and the evangelicals of the Second Great Awakening—chief among them, evangelist Charles Finney.

Our world has been shaped by people who revered Christian truths and absolute moral values over feelings and emotions. Today, unfortunately, the Christian faith gets little credit for the great strides of advancement it has inspired. In fact, Christianity is frequently impugned as an irrational "superstition" that can only be accepted on an emotional basis.

For example, the feminist writer and ACLU attorney Wendy Kaminer writes, "Ours is an evangelical culture. So many people convinced that they've been saved by Jesus, abused by Satanists, cured by homeopathy or the laying on of hands, abducted by aliens, or protected by angels seek public acknowledgment that their convictions are true.... Generally, the only proof offered for a fantastic belief is the passion it inspires in believers. It is usually futile to ask for more."[5]

Now, that is a serious charge—but before we become defensive, we should acknowledge that, yes, there are some Christians who seem to reduce the Christian faith to an ecstatic emotional experience. There are churches that preach faith as an irrational belief system which defies logic. There are some believers who offer no more evidence for the claims of Christ than an excess of emotion.

So it is up to us as Christians to demonstrate to the world that ours is a reasonable faith, founded upon rational evidence. As we demonstrate a sane, reasoned worldview, we can lead the fight for a return to rationality in our media, our government, our schools, and every other institution of our society. Let's look at some specific ways we can help restore reason and truth to the world around us.

Restoring Sanity to the Media

The late British journalist Malcolm Muggeridge (1903-1990) was an agnostic for most of his life. Early in his career, as a Moscow correspondent for the *Manchester Guardian*, he was sympathetic to communism. He converted to Christ in his late sixties and wrote a number of books on faith.

Muggeridge once noted that if he needed forgiveness for anything, it was for the sin of being "fatally fluent." He was such a gifted writer that he could take absolute nonsense and make it sound like brilliant reasoning. He was deeply remorseful that he had spent the bulk of his career using his "fatally fluent" talent to manipulate the opinions of millions of readers.[6]

Today, there are thousands of "fatally fluent" print and broadcast journalists and commentators in the news business. They are so talented and glib they could sell ice cubes to polar bears. They have no conscience about misleading their audience. With their postmodern worldview, they don't believe in "truth" anyway. All that matters to them is that their side wins, even if it means twisting the truth and manipulating emotions.

Many news consumers are aware of manipulation in the news media, but they ask, "What can I do? I'm just one person." Yet there is a great deal that one person can do, and if we combine the efforts of many viewers we can have a positive effect. Here are some suggestions:

1. Question everything you read, see, and hear in the media. Be aware that most news stories contain at least some innocent factual errors, some unconscious bias, and possibly even deliberate distortion.

   If a news story damages someone's reputation, remind yourself that the story may not be true. It is wise to suspend judgment until all the facts are in. Don't just scan headlines—*read the stories*. Sometimes headlines are misleading.

   Some examples: In 2007, one popular online news site carried a couple of misleading headlines: "Three Illegal Immigrants Shot Dead Crossing U.S. Border: Police," and, "U.S., Iraqi Troops Clash in Baghdad." What do these headlines tell us? At first glance you would naturally assume that American law enforcement officers killed illegal immigrants as they tried to enter the U.S., and that American and Iraqi troops shot at each other in Baghdad. Wrong on both counts. The illegal immigrants were killed by bandits from Mexico. The U.S. and Iraqi forces fought side-by-side against Sunni insurgents.

In early 2010, an Ohio newspaper carried the headline "Utah Bill Criminalizes Miscarriage." Now, that is a shocking headline. It suggests that, in the state of Utah, if a woman suffers a complication in pregnancy and loses her fetus, she could be arrested and treated as a criminal. But that is absolutely untrue. When you read the story, you find out that Utah has passed a law in response to a case in which a young woman, seven months pregnant, paid a man to give her a severe beating in order to cause her to miscarry. The Utah law does not affect complications of pregnancy. It does not even affect legal abortions. It is intended to prevent reckless and violent behavior that would result in a miscarriage.

Also in early 2010, an online news website carried the headline "Tim Tebow 'Nazi Rally.'" Tim Tebow is a football player who is famous for his outspoken Christian witness and his exemplary behavior. So this headline suggests that a Christian football player attended a "Nazi rally" and it has quite a bit of shock value. But if you click on the headline and read the story, you find that the headline was misleading. The article was about a party Mr. Tebow held to celebrate being drafted into the NFL. A number of sportswriters attended the party, including one who apparently didn't think there was enough boozing and carousing for his tastes—so he made a foolish joke about the party being "like some kind of Nazi rally." The sportswriter later apologized for the remark—but the damage was done.

2. If you don't want to be manipulated and misled, *read the entire article*, not just the headline. When you read the whole article, be skeptical. Don't necessarily believe everything you read.

3. Do your homework. Biased and dishonest reporters count on news consumers being too lazy to check their facts. Use Google or the public library to fact-check the claims of journalists. Examine all sides of every issue.

4. Know the difference between reporting and editorializing. It is okay for columnists and editors to express their opinions on the Opinion Page.

But it is *not* okay for reporters to slip their opinions into news stories. Even though many postmodern journalists claim that slanting the news is now acceptable, it is a deceptive and manipulative practice. Learn to spot bias and distortion in the stories you read and hear.

5. Contact journalists and editors with your concerns. Online news articles often include an email address for feedback. When writing, be brief and courteous—and be a good Christian witness. Offer a fair critique of both the positive and negative points. Who knows? By expressing your views, you may trigger a retraction or a more balanced report in the future.

6. Write letters. When a news outlet reports fairly on an issue, write and express your gratitude. If that news outlet gets it wrong, speak up. If you write to a TV network about its news coverage, send a copy of that letter to your local affiliate. Local stations need to hear from their audience if the network they carry offends viewers on a regular basis.

7. Talk about media bias with your friends. Avoid getting into arguments, but don't hesitate to speak up and help raise people's consciousness about the way the media uses emotion to manipulate opinions.

8. If you are a young person, consider a career in the media. If possible, find Christian mentors in the news industry who can advise you, encourage you, and pray with you for boldness and opportunities. If you are a parent, teacher, youth leader, or pastor, encourage young people to consider a career in print or broadcast journalism. Support them and pray for them, because a career in the news industry is not easy for people of faith.

We cannot afford to surrender any segment of our society to the secularists. We must ask God to raise up strong believers who will join the ranks of the media and claim that industry for Christ. Only by sending people of strong faith and strong principles into that segment of society can we begin to restore sanity to the media.

Restoring Sanity to the Government

Government at every level—from the school board and city council to the federal level—is geared toward accommodating the feelings of pressure groups and interest groups. Yet, in the postmodern mindset, there are still *some* people whose feelings may be safely disregarded by all levels of government: Christians.

In the spring of 2006, more than 25,000 evangelical Christian young people gathered in San Francisco for a two-day "Battle Cry for a Generation" rally. The event was led by Ron Luce, founder of the Texas-based Teen Mania ministry. It was billed as a Christian "reverse rebellion" against a corrupt popular culture which promotes immorality and drug abuse among our nation's young people.

Government officials in San Francisco were aghast at this invasion of Jesus-worshiping, morality-minded young people from around the country. State assemblyman Mark Leno stood before City Hall and condemned the Christian youth, saying, "They're loud, they're obnoxious, they're disgusting, and they should get out of San Francisco." The Board of Supervisors even passed a resolution condemning the event as an "act of provocation" by an "anti-gay," "anti-choice" organization, intended to "negatively influence the politics of America's most tolerant and progressive city."[7]

For some reason, the Board of Supervisors didn't even see the irony in their statement. By passing that resolution, the city fathers made it clear that they were only "tolerant" of people and ideas they agree with, but they were hostile and intolerant toward Christians. What kind of "tolerance" is that?

But, of course, the feelings of Christians don't matter.

Over the years, we have seen many decisions by school administrators and courts restricting the First Amendment rights of Christians. The courts have barred student-led prayer before football games. Valedictorians are prevented from expressing their faith and moral values in commencement speeches. A federal court ruled that the Pledge of Allegiance, with the phrase "one nation under God," could not be recited in public schools (the case is still pending). Most of these cases are provoked by the ACLU.

As Christians, we don't ask the government to bend over backwards out of sensitivity to our feelings. Here are some suggestions:

- Ask that our government obey the Constitution and principles of fairness and equal justice under the law. So, whenever government at any level engages in actions and decisions that offend our values and our faith, we have a moral duty to speak up. And we must speak words of grace and truth, words of Christ-like gentleness but also Christ-like boldness. We are called by God's Word to be good citizens, obedient to the laws and authorities that govern us. After all, in a democratic republic, *we are the government.* We elect our leaders, and our leaders represent us and are accountable to us. We must demand principled, rational government—a government focused on the serious challenges of this world, not one which merely panders to people's emotions in order to maintain its own power.

  This means that, as citizens and voters, we need to think clearly and rationally about the issues and candidates we support. We need to listen carefully to what politicians say—and what they don't say. When politicians evade tough questions about important policy issues, write or call them. Be cordial and respectful, but tell your representative you want forthright answers to important questions.

- Learn to recognize when politicians and candidates try to manipulate your emotions in speeches or with political ads. Some will use fear tactics to scare you into voting for them. Others will use pleasant images and soothing music to lull you into voting for them. Lawmakers will often attach warm-fuzzy names to legislation, such as "The Protect Our Kids and Little Puppies Act" or "The Mom and Apple Pie Bill." But buried in the fine print of the legislation are earmarks, tax hikes, pork-barrel spending, and other nasty items that are neither warm nor fuzzy.

- Don't let politicians manipulate you through your emotions. Do your homework. Be informed. Demand that politicians be accountable.

Restoring Sanity to Our Education System

A Canadian teen named McKenzie had to watch *An Inconvenient Truth* four times—once in World History class, again in Economics, again in World Issues, and finally in Ecology. McKenzie—an actual high school student, though his name has been changed—couldn't understand why four different teachers showed him the same film. "I've spoken to the principal about it," he told a correspondent for the *National Post* of Canada, "and he said that teachers are instructed to present it as a debate. But every time we've seen it, well, one teacher said this is basically a two-sided debate, but this movie really gives you the best idea of what's going on." He adds that most of his classmates "don't know there's another side to the argument."

McKenzie's mother was displeased. "This is just being poured into kids' brains," she said, instead of letting them know there's a debate going on. An educational system falls down when they start taking one side."[8]

An Inconvenient Truth is required viewing in schools and universities across the United States and England. At Roger Williams University in Bristol, Rhode Island, some students are required to view *An Inconvenient Truth* in order to receive their degree. Jeffrey Hughes, assistant dean of marine and natural sciences, defended the requirement, saying, "Scientists no longer question whether the atmosphere is being warmed due to human activities…. There is no doubt that we're warming the earth."[9]

That is a statement of bias, not a statement of scientific fact. Some of the film's science advisors admit that *An Inconvenient Truth* has serious flaws. University of Colorado climatologist Kevin Vranes says that the film is guilty of "overselling our certainty about knowing the future." NASA scientist James E. Hansen worries about the way the film blames extreme hurricane activity on global warming. "We need to be more careful in describing the hurricane story than he is," Hanson says.

An Inconvenient Truth claims that 2005—the year before the film was released—was the warmest year since records have been kept. *Wrong*: Temperatures have been falling since 1998. The film makes an emotional appeal about polar bears becoming extinct. *Wrong*: Polar bear populations are steadily growing. The film appeals to viewers' fears, claiming that sea levels will rise up to twenty feet, flooding coastal cities. *Wrong*: The International Panel on Climate Change predicts that average sea levels will change a few inches at most.[10]

In England, when the government decreed that all secondary schools had to show *An Inconvenient Truth*, a group in Kent filed suit to stop the government plan. The judge found that *An Inconvenient Truth* contained nine significant factual errors, some of which created an emotionally charged atmosphere of "alarmism and exaggeration." The judge did not block showing the film, but did require the use of a discussion guide to provide balance to the film's "one-sided" presentation.[11]

Now, why is this important? So what if *An Inconvenient Truth* contains inaccuracies? Shouldn't we still want to recycle and clean up the air? Of course we should. But it's wrong to frighten school kids with a "truth" that is not only "inconvenient" but untrue and emotionally manipulative. In fact, a recent survey of 1,150 children between ages seven and eleven revealed that half of those young children feel anxious and worried about global warming, and many are even losing sleep. They expressed fear about potential health consequences to themselves or their pets, and worries about the inundation of cities.[12]

Though global warming alarmists claim that the issue of climate change has been "settled" by "scientific consensus," there are many scientists who disagree. The Petition Project has gathered signatures from 31,000 scientists, including more than 9,000 Ph.D.s in such fields as climatology, environment, and earth science—all of whom challenge the claim that human-produced greenhouse gases are damaging the planet. Those 9,000 Ph.D. scientists represent fifteen times more scientists than have participated in the United Nations' Intergovernmental Panel on Climate Change—the organization behind the climate change agenda. A spokesman for The Petition Project noted, "The very large number of petition signers demonstrates that, if there is a consensus among American scientists, it is in *opposition* to the human-caused global warming hypothesis rather than in favor of it."[13]

Emotions run high on both sides of the global warming debate. But questions of climate change cannot be resolved by emotions. You undoubtedly have an opinion on the issue. But let me ask you this: On what do you base your opinion? Sound bites heard on TV? A viewing of *An Inconvenient Truth*? Here's a suggestion: Read two substantive, authoritative books on global warming—one pro and one con. Exercise your intellect, examine the best arguments on both sides, and make up your own mind. Then you won't just have an opinion—you'll have an *informed* opinion.

Armed with information, you can speak intelligently to your children about the issue. If their school shows them *An Inconvenient Truth*, you can help them put the information in perspective. You can help them deal with any worries they may have for pets, polar bears, or themselves.

What's more, you can talk intelligently to your children's teachers, principal, or school board regarding what you think is the best way to present this issue to students. Armed with the arguments from both sides of the issue, you will be able to speak knowledgeably and confidently.

Here are some tips to help you have a positive impact on your children's school—not just with regard to environmental issues, but with any and all issues that may arise in your children's education:

> *Be aware.* Remember, as we saw in Chapter 5, there are many educators who are trying to use your children's emotions to "challenge" and reshape their beliefs. Be attuned to what your children are being taught, and the methods used to teach them.

> *Be alert.* If you hear your child referring to a classroom activity that is focused on feelings—such as a "worry box" or a "feelings tree"—don't panic. Find out more. Ask your child about the activity, but avoid getting upset in front of your child. Talk to your child's teacher and find out what the activity involves.

> *Be controlled.* When talking to teachers and administrators, always remain calm and reasonable. Avoid jumping to conclusions. Make sure you have all the facts before you express your opinion. Don't just complain when things go wrong—affirm and praise educators when things go right.

Get involved. If you find that your child's school is tampering with his or her feelings, values, opinions, and beliefs, then talk to other concerned parents. A coalition of parents carries more weight than one family acting alone. If need be, consider removing your child from that school and placing your child in a private Christian school. if you think you're qualified, explore the possibility of home schooling. Your first concern must be the wellbeing of your child.

Empower your child. Train your child to be a witness and a role model at school. Pray with your child, teach him or her the Scriptures, and encourage your child to speak openly about faith in Christ.

Pray for your child. Every day, when you send your child to school, ask for God's protection over your child. Pray throughout the day. Go into your children's bedroom at night and pray over them as they sleep. Ask God to armor-plate your children every day against the attacks of Satan and this fallen world.

Our mission as followers of Christ is to protect and defend the minds of our children and, as God gives us grace, to restore our little piece of the world to sanity.

Restoring Families and Churches to Sanity

The Bible tells us "Great peace have they who love your law, and nothing can make them stumble" (Psalm 119:165). Here then are some sound principles for keeping our families and churches from stumbling:

1. Know *what* you believe and *why* you believe. Study the Scriptures. Learn how to explain to others why you believe that the Bible is God's revealed truth, why you believe in the historical reality of the resurrection, and why you are confident of your eternal destiny in heaven with the Father. Even though the cross may be disappearing from the landscape around you, make sure the cross is planted firmly, immovably in your life and your family life.

2. Pray for the leaders and teachers in your church. Pray for opportunities to exercise your spiritual gifts in your church, your neighborhood, your school, and your workplace.

3. 3. Encourage your pastors and teachers. Send notes of affirmation to your teachers and leaders. Mention specific teachings that have impacted your life. Encourage more teaching on the Bible, the cross of Christ, and principles of the faith.

4. Get involved. Volunteer to teach classes or lead Bible studies in your church. Remember, God did not intend church members to be spectators. Every member is to be a minister and an evangelist. Your pastor's job is to equip the saints (that's you!) for the work of the ministry.

5. In your family and your church, make sure every decision and action is based on biblical truth—not emotions, not feelings, not indulging your weaknesses and impulses. When disagreements arise, when decisions must be made, when sin must be addressed, gather your family or church family together, search the Scriptures, and find God's solution to those issues.

6. Make time for family devotions. If you are too busy to spend regular time reading the Scriptures and praying with your family, you are too busy, period.

7. Encourage intellectual pursuits. Study the Scriptures together. Turn off the TV and read. Involve your family in mealtime discussions of issues and events. Thoughtfully apply God's truth to these discussions. When your family watches a TV show or movie, take time to discuss the implications of that program. Did the creators of that program appeal to the viewers' intellect—or emotions? What were the biases, assumptions, and hidden messages in that show? Help your kids become aware of the media's attempt to influence their opinions through emotional manipulation.

8. When it is necessary to correct or discipline your children, do so in a calm, reasonable manner. When you apply consequences to your children's poor choices and poor behavior, explain to them that you

are following the principles of God's Word, not lashing out in anger. Help your kids to see the difference between acting out of emotion and acting in a reasoned and principled way. The next time your kids throw a tantrum, don't shout back. Try *lowering* your voice. By doing so, your child has to become quiet in order to hear what you are saying. You de-escalate the emotions of the conflict. You show your child who is in control. You demonstrate that reason is a more effective problem-solver than emotion. Remember that whenever you must discipline your kids, you have an opportunity to *disciple* them. The words "disciple" and "discipline" both come from the Latin root word *discipulus*, which means someone who has been trained and instructed for a purpose. So always seek to disciple your kids—especially when you have to discipline them.

9. Never forget the solid foundation of your faith. The Christian church began with an empty cross—and an empty tomb. This was an historic event in time and space. Jesus of Nazareth lived, died on the cross—then walked out of the tomb alive. Five hundred witnesses saw Him, spoke to Him, touched Him, broke bread with Him, and knew Him for who He was. One of those witnesses—the man known as Doubting Thomas—saw Him and said, "My Lord and my God!" The Christian church first met in Jerusalem, the city where Jesus died and rose again. His tomb was the property of one of Jerusalem's most prominent citizens, a member of the Sanhedrin named Joseph of Arimathea. Anyone who wished to examine the evidence for the resurrection simply had to walk out the city gates to the tomb of Joseph and personally inspect the site. Many people undoubtedly did so. The Christian faith spread rapidly because people were convinced by the evidence for the resurrection. The empty tomb was incontrovertible proof of the central fact of the Gospel: Jesus lives! Two thousand years later, that unassailable fact is still the foundation of our faith.

10. Never forget your destiny. Unfortunately, many Christians seem to have lost sight of their heavenly home. Many of us have a hard

time imagining what heaven will be like, so we simply avoid thinking about it. What a tragedy! Heaven is the vision of the future Jesus gave to inspire us and encourage us in our walk with Him. He told us He was going to prepare a place for us, and He intended that we keep our eyes fixed on our destiny.

The Scriptures tell us, "He has made everything beautiful in its time. He has also set eternity in the hearts of men; yet they cannot fathom what God has done from beginning to end" (Ecclesiastes 3:11). Heaven is in our hearts. We long for it. We were made for heaven. The great tragedy of our lives is that we have failed to focus our thoughts on heaven.

The Bible depicts heaven as a concrete reality—a place with buildings and gardens and flowing rivers. We will have whole, resurrection bodies—just like the body of Jesus after His resurrection. Following the resurrection, He appeared to His disciples and said, "Look at my hands and my feet. It is I myself! Touch me and see; a ghost does not have flesh and bones, as you see I have" (Luke 24:39). The apostle Paul tells us that the Lord Jesus "will transform our lowly bodies so that they will be like his glorious body" (Philippians 3:21).

We will live on a new Earth, which God promised to us in the Old and New Testaments. God told Isaiah, "Behold, I will create new heavens and a new earth" (Isaiah 65:17a). And John wrote, "Then I saw a new heaven and a new earth, for the first heaven and the first earth had passed away" (Revelation 21:1). Our dwelling place on this new earth will be a great city, brilliantly designed by the Master Architect, a place of peace, light, and endless fellowship. God wanted us to know that this heavenly city is no poetic metaphor, so he gave us its exact dimensions in Revelation 21:15-17.

Heaven is an objective reality. It is the destiny that lies ahead of you. No matter how intense the opposition you face, no matter how difficult the obstacles in your path, if you keep your eyes fixed on heaven, you will always be moving in God's direction.

The One Who Gave His Blood

Charles Colson tells a story that underscores the contrast between a culture driven by emotion and a culture ruled by truth and principle. The story takes place in northern Iraq, during a time when the insurgency was at its height and the nation was torn by irrational violence and senseless rage.

Two Iraqi insurgents placed a roadside bomb with the intention of killing American soldiers. Their plan was thwarted when they were observed and fired on by an Army helicopter. When the shooting stopped, the insurgents were seriously wounded but alive. Medevac helicopters landed, picked up the wounded insurgents, and flew them to an Army hospital at Camp Speicher, near Tikrit.

One of the Iraqis needed thirty pints of blood or he would die. Blood reserves at the hospital were low. A series of major trauma cases had reduced the hospital's blood supply to its last few pints.

The hospital sent out a call for volunteer donors. Within minutes, a long line of soldiers assembled, ready to give blood. A reporter asked the soldier at the head of the line if it mattered to him that his blood would be given to the enemy—to a man who was trying to kill Americans.

"No," the soldier said simply. "A human life is a human life." This man was ready to give life to a man who was trying to take life. Reflecting on the stark difference between the American soldier and the Iraqi insurgent, Colson wrote:

I have never seen a more dramatic example of worldviews in contrast, nor have I been prouder of an American G.I. On one hand, we have the horrors of a civilization that values death—even the death of its own children—if by killing them they can hurt the infidels. On the other side, we have a story that makes us realize just how deeply embedded within American life is our Judeo-Christian heritage. This heritage teaches that human life is sacred—even the life of an enemy who falls into our hands.[14]

We follow the One who gave His blood for His enemies, who bled to death on a cross for those who were driven by hatred and sin. We were once His enemies. Now, because of that cross, He calls us "friends."

We follow the One who restores sanity to a world gone mad, who gives life to a world lost in death and sin. He still shows love to His enemies, to those who are hell-bent on erasing His cross from the world. He still says, "Forgive those who hate Me, who hate My cross, for they don't know what they are doing."

Let us enthrone Him as King of our emotions and passions. Let us make Him the Lord of our thoughts and imagination, our plans and intentions. And let us make Him the Lord of our intellect and our lives.

As He told us in His Word, love the Lord your God with all your heart. Love Him with all your soul. Love Him with all your strength. And yes, *love Him with all your mind.*

Epilogue

In a message to Congress on December 1, 1862, President Abraham Lincoln warned, "We shall nobly save, or meanly lose, the last best hope of earth."

President Lincoln's warning has never been more urgent than it is today.

I think many people have a false sense of security, thinking that America is invulnerable because of her strong economy, strong military, and strong traditions. As much as I love America, I think she could be swept into the dustbin of history within our lifetime—and I believe it *will* happen if we allow it.

As a loyal adopted son of this land, and as someone who deeply loves and reveres America's history, I mourn what I am witnessing today. I see my beloved land succumbing to moral decay. I see this "last best hope of earth" at the brink of an abyss. Her citizens, mesmerized by feelings, are mindlessly pushing her toward that brink.

David M. Walker served as United States Comptroller General from 1998 to 2008. In his book *Comeback America*, Walker warns that the end of the American civilization could be approaching more quickly than we imagine:

> Perhaps because we are a young country, Americans tend not to pay much attention to the lessons of history. Well, we should start, because those lessons are brutal....
>
> Many of us think that a super-powerful, prosperous nation like America will be a permanent fixture dominating the world scene. We are too big to fail. But you don't have to delve far into the history books to see what has happened to other once-dominant powers.... Great powers rise and fall.... The millennium of the Roman Empire—

which included five hundred years as a republic—came to an end in the fifth century after scores of years of gradual decay....

America presents unsettling parallels with the disintegration of Rome—a decline of moral values, a loss of political civility, an overextended military, an inability to control national borders, and the growth of fiscal irresponsibility by the central government. Do these sound familiar?[1]

Historian Niall Ferguson is the author of *Colossus: The Rise And Fall Of The American Empire*. He warns that when an empire collapses, its demise happens swiftly, often violently, and almost always without warning. He points to the fall of the Roman Empire as a prime example:

What is most striking about this history is the speed of the Roman Empire's collapse. In just five decades, the population of Rome itself fell by three-quarters. Archaeological evidence from the late fifth century—inferior housing, more primitive pottery, fewer coins, smaller cattle—shows that the benign influence of Rome diminished rapidly in the rest of western Europe.... "The end of civilization" came within the span of a single generation.

Other great empires have suffered comparably swift collapses.... [Empires] function in apparent equilibrium for some unknowable period. And then, quite abruptly, they collapse.... The shift... to destruction and then to desolation is not cyclical. It is sudden.[2]

Civilizations rise on a foundation of moral strength. When the foundation crumbles, that civilization is doomed to fail. The swift and sudden collapse of the Roman Empire was not so much the result of invasions by the barbarian Vandals and Visigoths, but the result of moral decay and internal corruption.

Historian Will Durant (1885–1981) summed up the fall of Rome in these words: "A great civilization is not conquered from without until it has destroyed itself within. The essential causes of Rome's decline lay in her people, her morals, her class struggle, her failing trade, her bureaucratic despotism, her stifling taxes, her consuming wars."[3]

Substitute just one word in that last sentence—and the result is chilling: *The essential causes of America's decline lay in her people, her morals, her class struggle, her failing trade, her bureaucratic despotism, her stifling taxes, her consuming wars.* We see all of these forces straining the fabric of our society today. But none is more destructive to America's soul than the decline of her morals and her spiritual life. In just a few chilling words, Will Durant has sketched for us a glimpse of our own future—when the crosses are gone.

Muslim extremists clearly see the parallel between the decline and fall of the Roman Empire and the present decline of the West. Many Muslim leaders and thinkers have told me they are convinced that the decline and fall of the West shall be the result of the inevitable failure of Christianity. As Christianity disintegrates, they tell me, it will create a spiritual vacuum in the West—and their extreme brand of Islam will rush in to fill that void.

Islamists make no secret of the fact that they seek world domination. They are disciplined and relentless in pursuit of their goals. They don't expect to confront the West in open warfare. They believe Western civilization will become so decadent that, like the Roman Empire, America will collapse like a house of cards. Just as the Vandals and Visigoths sacked a weak and dispirited Rome in the fifth century A.D., the Islamists of the 21st century are waiting for the Christian West to collapse so they can move in unopposed.

One of the more thoughtful intellectuals of the Muslim world told me, "Islam spread throughout the Middle East and North Africa by the sword. But Western culture will be handed to us on a platter. The people of the West are led about by their feelings and sentimentality. They are ruled by their passions. Soft and undisciplined, they are no match for the determined soldiers of Islam. The West will fall into our hands like overripe fruit."

I fear there may be truth in his prediction. The culture of the West has forsaken reason and moral principles in favor of an unthinking, emotion-based mindset. We have replaced moral values with moral relativism. We tolerate anything *except* God's truth. We extol freedom of speech and thought—as long as those thoughts don't derive from Scripture. And this feelings-based mindset may well be our undoing.

Is there no hope? Is our civilization doomed to collapse?

As social critic Charles Krauthammer once said, "The question of whether America is in decline cannot be answered yes or no. There is no yes or no. Both answers are wrong, because the assumption that somehow there exists some predetermined inevitable trajectory... is wrong. Nothing is inevitable. Nothing is written. For America today, decline is not a condition. Decline is a choice."[4]

The decision rests with us. We choose whether America—and indeed all of Western civilization—rises or falls. Our generation—you and I and all of our fellow citizens—will make the decision.

And the decision turns on what you and I decide to do with the cross of Christ. Will we stand by it? Will we defend it boldly and unashamedly? Will we live by the commandments of our crucified Lord? Will we proclaim His love and His life to the world around us? Will we be salt and light to a corrupt and increasingly dark world?

Today, before the crosses are gone, we must choose. There is only one rational choice, my friend. There is only one decision for us to make.

We must choose the cross of Christ.

Notes

Chapter One: The Dangerous, Offensive Cross

1. Ariane de Vogue, "Supreme Court Keeps Mojave Cross Case Alive," ABC News, April 28, 2010, http://abcnews.go.com/Politics/Supreme_Court/ supreme-court-refuses-ban-mojave-cross/story?id=9536679.

2. Suzy Platt, editor, *Respectfully Quoted: A Dictionary of Quotations Requested from the Congressional Research Service*, Washington D.C.: Library of Congress, 1989, Bartleby.com, 2003, www.bartleby.com/73/.

3. Paul Kengor: "25 Years after the Pope and Ronald Reagan Met in Rome," History News Network, June 7, 2007, http://hnn.us/roundup/ comments/39834.html.

4. ACLJ press release, "ACLJ Sues Alabama School District After It Threatens Disciplinary Action Against Student Who Wears Cross Necklace," ACLJ. org, October 12, 2000, http://www.aclj.org/News/Read.aspx?ID=239.

5. Drew Zahn, "U.S. Lawmakers Defend 'In God We Trust,'" WorldNetDaily, November 16, 2009, http://www.aclj.org/News/Read.aspx?ID=3515; Rick Tyler, " Capitol Visitor Center Report: Reconstructing American History," Renewing American Leadership, December 12, 2008, http://action.afa. net/uploadedFiles/Activism/AFA_Action_Alerts/cvcreport.pdf?n=9711; Staff of Senator Jim DeMint, "DeMint CVC Amendment Accepted," U.S. Senate Website, July 7, 2009, http://demint.senate.gov/public/index. cfm?p=JimsBlog&Label_id=9f67bb12-5645-4c68-be0d-ecfc47587aca.

6. Dennis Prager, "Taliban Come to Los Angeles," Townhall.com, June 8, 2006, http://townhall.com/columnists/DennisPrager/2004/06/08/ taliban_come_to_los_angeles.

7. Author uncredited, "Welcome to Los Angeles: The History of Los Angeles County," LAAvenue.com, http://www.laavenue.com/LAHistory.htm.

8. Prager, ibid.

9. BBC, "Woman to Sue BA in Necklace Row," BBC News, October 15, 2006, http://news.bbc.co.uk/2/hi/uk_news/england/london/6052608.stm; Jonathan Petre and David Millward, "BA's Climbdown Follows Tirade from Archbishop," London *Daily Telegraph*, November 25, 2006, http://www.telegraph.co.uk/news/uknews/1535099/BAs-climbdown-follows-tirade-from-archbishop.html; Robert Spencer, " British Airways: Cross No, Hijab Yes," Jihad Watch, October 14, 2006, http://www.jihadwatch.org/2006/10/british-airways-cross-no-hijab-yes.html.

10. Author uncredited, "College Removes Cross—From Chapel," WorldNetDaily.com, October 27, 2006, http://www.wnd.com/?pageId=38577.

11. Fox News and Associated Press, "Some William and Mary College Alumni Hold Back Donations After Cross Removal," Fox News Channel, February 05, 2007, http://www.foxnews.com/story/0,2933,250340,00.html.

12. Author uncredited, "College Prez Backtracks on Cross Removal," WorldNetDaily.com, December 22, 2006, http://www.wnd.com/?pageId=39392.

13. Jeff Johnson, "Christian Churches Should Stop Using the Cross, Group Says," Crosswalk.com, August 22, 2003, http://www.crosswalk.com/1216019/.

14. John R. W. Stott, *The Cross of Christ* (Downers Grove, Ill.: InterVarsity Press, 1986), pp. 329, 335.

15. Max Lucado, *He Chose the Nails* (Nashville: Thomas Nelson, 2000), 113.

16. James Thrower, *Marxist-Leninist "Scientific Atheism" and the Study of Religion and Atheism in the USSR* (Berlin: Walter de Gruyter & Co., 1983), 460.

17. Thomas Jefferson, "Jefferson's Letter to the Danbury Baptists: The Final Letter, as Sent," January 1, 1802, Library of Congress, http://www.loc.gov/loc/lcib/9806/danpre.html.

18. Bridget Levitz, "Church Rights Being Argued—Action by Parks Board May Be Unconstitutional," *Elkhart (Indiana) Truth*, October 29, 2006, http://www.aclj.org/News/Read.aspx?ID=2435.

19. Hillary Rodham Clinton, "Remarks on the Human Rights Agenda for the 21st Century," Georgetown University's Gaston Hall, Washington, D.C., December 14, 2009, http://www.state.gov/secretary/rm/2009a/12/133544.htm.

20. Charles Colson, "Two-Minute Warning: Freedom of Worship—An Anorexic Description of Our Rights," Colson Center, June 30, 2010, http://www.colsoncenter.org/the-center/the-chuck-colson-center/two-minute-warning (online video transcribed by the author, July 7, 2010).

Chapter Two: Feelings vs. Facts

1. Mike Allen with Matthew L. Wald, "Maneuver by Kennedy's Plane Suggests He Was Disoriented," *The New York Times*, July 21, 1999, retrieved at http://query.nytimes.com/gst/fullpage.html?res=9F03E3DD163EF932A1 5754C0A96F958260; Carl H. Lavin, "How Student Pilots Are Drilled For Conditions Kennedy Saw," *The New York Times*, July 21, 1999, retrieved at http://query.nytimes.com/gst/fullpage.html?res=9A05E0DD163EF932A 15754C0A96F958260; Phaedra Hise, "JFK Jr.'s Fatal Mistakes," *Salon*, July 15, 2000, retrieved at http://archive.salon.com/news/feature/2000/07/15/ntsb/index.html.

2. Richard Corliss, "Our Critic Rides A Time Machine," Time, February 10, 1997, retrieved at http://www.time.com/time/magazine/article/0,9171,985897,00.html.

3. Bob Spitz, *The Beatles: The Biography* (New York: Little Brown & Co., 2006), pp. 705-735, *passim.*

4. David Viscott, *Finding Your Strength in Difficult Times* (New York: McGraw-Hill Professional, 2003), 195.

5. Lynn Rasmussen, *Men are Easy, A Simple Guide to Fun, Sexy, Happy, and Easy Relationships* (Makwao, Maui, HI: Mohala Media, LLC., 2007), 33.

6. Angela McGlowan, *Bamboozled: How Americans Are Being Exploited by the Lies of the Liberal Agenda* (Nashville: Thomas Nelson, 2007), pp. 6, 13-14.

7. Bert Decker, *You Got to Be Believed to Be Heard* (Updated Edition, New York: St. Martin's Press, 2008), 39.

8. Decker, 38.

9. Ravi Zacharias, Address to the United Nations' Prayer Breakfast, October 30, 2007, retrieved at http://www.rzim.org/GlobalElements/ GFV/tabid/449/ArticleID/96/CBModuleId/1045/Default.aspx.

10. Robert Lightner, *The God of the Bible and Other Gods* (Grand Rapids: Kregel Publications, 1998), 203.

11. George Barna, "Americans Are Most Likely to Base Truth on Feelings," Barna Research Group, February 12, 2002, retrieved at http://www. barna.org/FlexPage.aspx?Page=BarnaUpdate&BarnaUpdateID=106

12. Ravi Zacharias, ibid.

13. Al Gore, quoted by John A. Marini and Ken Masugi, eds., *The Progressive Revolution in Politics and Political Science: Transforming the American Regime* (Lanham, MD: Rowman & Littlefield, 2005), 277.

14. B. A. Robinson, "How Judges and Justices Interpret the U.S. Constitution and Laws," ReligiousTolerance.org, May 18, 2007, retrieved at http:// www.religioustolerance.org/scotuscon6.htm.

Chapter Three: Restoring Sanity to the Media

1. S. E. Cupp, *Losing Our Religion* (New York: Simon & Schuster, 2010), 80-81.

2. Ibid.

3. Garin K. Hovannisian, "The Weekly Standard vs. The New Republic: How One Blogging Soldier Started a War between Magazines," *The New York Review of Magazines*, Columbia University Graduate School of Journalism, 2008, retrieved at http://www.nyrm.org/Features/ FeatureHovannisian.html; Michael Goldfarb, "The Blog: Fact or Fiction?," *The Weekly Standard*, July 18, 2007, retrieved at http://www. weeklystandard.com/weblogs/TWSFP/2007/07/fact_or_fiction_1.asp; John Cook, "Dossier: The New Republic's Soldier's Tale," RadarOnline. com, January 22, 2008, retrieved at http://www.radaronline.com/ exclusives/2008/01/scott-beauchamp-new-republic-documents-

foia.php; Howard Kurtz, "Army Concludes Baghdad Diarist Accounts Untrue," *The Washington Post*, August 8, 2007, C01, retrieved at http://www.washingtonpost.com/wp-dyn/content/article/2007/08/07/AR2007080701922.html; Franklin Foer, "Fog of War: The Story of our Baghdad Diarist," *The New Republic*, December 10, 2007, retrieved at http://www.tnr.com/politics/story.html?id=51f6dc92-7f1d-4d5b-aebe-94668b7bfb32&p=1.

4. Jay Price and Qasim Zein, "Iraqi Cemetery's Business Falls," *The News & Observer* (Raleigh, NC), October 17, 2007, retrieved at http://www.newsobserver.com/505/story/738454.html.

5. Mitchell Stephens, "We're All Postmodern Now," *Columbia Journalism Review*, July/August 2005, retrieved at http://findarticles.com/p/articles/mi_qa3613/is_200507/ai_n14717888/pg_1?tag=artBody;col1.

6. Ibid.

7. Jack Shafer, "Fib Newton," *Slate*, October 29, 2002, retrieved at http://www.slate.com/?id=2073304; Jack Shafer, "The Jayson Blair Project," *Slate*, May 8, 2003, retrieved at http://www.slate.com/id/2082741/; CBS News, "Reporter Ousted For Deception: USA Today's Jack Kelley Misled Probe Of His Reporting," CBSNews.com, January 13, 2004, retrieved at http://www.cbsnews.com/stories/2004/01/13/national/main592892.shtml; Michelle Malkin, "Not Quite the News," MichelleMalkin.com, May 12, 2005, retrieved at http://michellemalkin.com/2005/05/12/not-quite-the-news/; Howard Kurtz, "Boston Globe Admits Freelancer's Story Included Fabrications," *The Washington Post*, April 16, 2005, retrieved at http://www.washingtonpost.com/wp-dyn/articles/A57908-2005Apr15.html; Howard Kurtz, "The Village Voice's No-Alternative News: Corporate Takeover," *The Washington Post*, October 24, 2005, retrieved at http://www.washingtonpost.com/wp-dyn/content/article/2005/10/23/AR2005102301504_pf.html; CNN Panel Discussion, "How Will ABC Anchor Swap Affect Ratings Battle?; Coverage of the Clintons' Marriage," CNN *Reliable Sources*, May 28, 2006, retrieved at http://transcripts.cnn.com/TRANSCRIPTS/0605/28/rs.01.html.

8. Bernard Goldberg, *Bias: A CBS Insider Exposes How the Media Distort the News* (Washington DC: Regnery, 2002). 127.

9. David Murray, Joel B. Schwartz, S. Robert Lichter, *It Ain't Necessarily So: How Media Make and Unmake the Scientific Picture of Reality* (Lanham, MD: Rowman & Littlefield, 2001), 29.

10. Goldberg, 121.

11. Jonathan Strong, "When McCain Picked Palin, Liberal Journalists Coordinated the Best Line of Attack," The Daily Caller, July 22, 2010, http://dailycaller.com/2010/07/22/when-mccain-picked-palin-liberal-journalists-coordinated-the-best-line-of-attack/.

12. David Gura, "Controversial Remarks About Limbaugh," NPR The Two-Way (NPR's News Blog), July 21, 2010, http://www.npr.org/blogs/thetwo-way/2010/07/21/128669697/comments-about-rush-limbaugh-cause-controversy.

13. Patrik Jonsson, "Journolist: Is 'Call Them Racists' a Liberal Media Tactic?," *Christian Science Monitor*, July 20, 2010, http://www.csmonitor.com/USA/Politics/2010/0720/JournoList-Is-call-them-racists-a-liberal-media-tactic.

14. Andrew Sullivan, "The Corruption Of JournoList," *The Atlantic*, July 20, 2010, http://andrewsullivan.theatlantic.com/the_daily_dish/2010/07/the-corruption-of-journolist.html.

15. Laura Ingraham, *Power to the People* (Washington, DC: Regnery, 2007), 162.

16. Alexander Solzhenitsyn, "Address at Harvard Class Day Afternoon Exercises," Harvard University, June 8, 1978, retrieved at http://www.columbia.edu/cu/augustine/arch/solzhenitsyn/harvard1978.html.

17. Mark Steyn, "Steynposts: Notes on a Show Trial," SteynOnline.com, June 8, 2008, retrieved at http://www.steynonline.com/content/blogsection/14/128/; Press Release, "Maclean's Responds to Recent Decision from the Canadian Human Rights Commission," Maclean's Magazine, June 26, 2008, retrieved at http://www.newswire.ca/en/releases/archive/June2008/26/c8368.html.

18. James Allan, "Canada's Deadly Tongue Trap," *The Australian*, June 6, 2008, retrieved at http://www.theaustralian.news.com.au/ story/0,25197,23816891-25192,00.html.

19. Andrew Bolt, "Free Speech Farce," *Herald Sun* (Melbourne, Australia), June 24, 2005, retrieved at http://www.news.com.au/heraldsun/ story/0,21985,15708881-25717,00.html; Mark Durie, "Daniel Scot's (In)credible Testimony," Saltshakers.org.au, retrieved at http://www. saltshakers.org.au/pdf/291222_DECISION__-_VCAT_CASE.pdf.

20. David Harrison, "Christian Preachers Face Arrest in Birmingham," *The Telegraph* (UK), June 2, 2008, retrieved at http://www.telegraph.co.uk/ news/uknews/2058935/Police-advise-Christian-preachers-to-leave-Muslin-area-of-Birmingham.html.

21. Michael Reagan, "Is This Our Future?," Townhall.com, June 4, 2008, retrievedathttp://townhall.com/Columnists/MichaelReagan/2008/06/04/ is_this_our_future; Jonathan Milne, "Anglican Priest, Canon Michael Ainsworth, Beaten Up in 'Faith Hate,'" *The Sunday Times* (London), March 15, 2008, retrieved at http://www.timesonline.co.uk/tol/comment/ faith/article3558715.ece.

22. Simon Walters, "We Are Biased, Admit the Stars of BBC News," *Mail on Sunday*, October 21, 2006, http://www.dailymail.co.uk/news/ article-411846/We-biased-admit-stars-BBC-News.html.

23. Chad Groening, "'Alternate Routes' to the Fairness Doctrine," OneNewsNow.com, August 21, 2009, http://www.onenewsnow.com/ Culture/Default.aspx?id=652322.

24. Brit Hume, "Tiger Woods Must Become Christian To Be Forgiven," *Fox News Sunday*, January 3, 2010, YouTube.com, online video viewed and transcribed by the authors on August 12, 2010, http://www.youtube.com/ watch?v=rgMr_Zc3OtA.

25. Tom Shales, "Brit Hume's Off Message: Have Faith, Tiger Woods, As Long As It's Christianity," *Washington Post*, January 5, 2010, http:// www.washingtonpost.com/wp-dyn/content/article/2010/01/04/ AR2010010403101.html.

26. Brad Wilmouth, "Olbermann: Hume Tried to 'Force' & 'Threaten' Tiger Woods into Christian Conversion," NewsBusters.org (Media Research Center), January 6, 2010, http://newsbusters.org/blogs/brad-wilmouth/2010/01/06/olbermann-hume-tried-force-threaten-tiger-woods-christian-conversion.

Chapter Four: Restoring Sanity to the Government
1. Todd Starnes, "Cop Tells Kids to Stop Praying at Supreme Court," ToddStarnes.com, http://toddstarnes.com/?p=776.
2. Todd Starnes, "National Anthem Banned at Lincoln Memorial?," ToddStarnes.com, http://toddstarnes.com/?p=798.
3. Abby Goodnough, " Behind Life-and-Death Fight, a Rift That Began Years Ago," *New York Times*, March 26, 2005, http://www.nytimes.com/2005/03/26/national/26families.html?ref=robert_schindler; Abby Goodnough, "Schiavo Dies, Ending Bitter Case Over Feeding Tube," *New York Times*, April 1, 2005, http://www.nytimes.com/2005/04/01/national/01schiavo.html?_r=1&ref=robert_schindler; Kathleen Antrim, "Terri Schiavo's Death Will Be an Atrocity," Newsmax, March 26, 2005, http://archive.newsmax.com/archives/articles/2005/3/26/35541.shtml.
4. Thomas Sowell, "War on Poverty Revisited," *Capitalism Magazine*, August 17, 2004, retrieved at http://www.capmag.com/article.asp?ID=3864.
5. Ibid.
6. Charles Murray, "The Underclass Revisited," The American Enterprise Institute for Public Policy Research, January 1, 2000, retrieved at http://www.aei.org/publications/pubID.14891/pub_detail.asp.
7. Michael Gryboski, "Answer to Poverty 'Complex,' Liberal Group Says," CNSNews.com, August 06, 2008, retrieved at http://www.cnsnews.com/public/content/article.aspx?RsrcID=33670.
8. Harry G. Shaffer, *American Capitalism and the Changing Role of Government*, (Westport, CT: Greenwood Publishing Group, 1999), 52.
9. "Offshore Information: Facts About Sweden," Asset Protection Corporation, retrieved at http://www.assetprotectioncorp.com/sweden.html.

10. Karlyn H. Bowman, et al, "Public Opinion on The War with Iraq," AEI Public Opinion Studies, American Enterprise Institute, January 11, 2007, retrieved at http://www.aei.org/docLib/20050805_IRAQ0805.pdf; Carl Kenneth Allard, *Warheads: Cable News and the Fog of War* (Annapolis, MD: Naval Institute Press, 2006), 113.

11. Jeff Glor, "Proposed Mosque Near Ground Zero Stokes Debate," CBS News, July 20, 2010, http://www.cbsnews.com/stories/2010/07/20/eveningnews/main6696724.shtml?tag=mncol;lst;2.

12. Tom Topousis, "Imam Terror Error," *New York Post*, June 19, 2010, http://www.nypost.com/p/news/local/manhattan/imam_terror_error_efmizkHuBUaVnfuQcrcabL.

13. Frank Walker, "We Must Act to End Jihad: Imam," *Sydney Sun-Herald*, March 21, 2004, http://www.smh.com.au/articles/2004/03/21/1079789939987.html.

14. Newt Gingrich, "Statement on Proposed Mosque/Islamic Community Center near Ground Zero," Newt.org, July 21, 2010, http://www.newt.org/newt-direct/newt-gingrich-statement-proposed-mosqueislamic-community-center-near-ground-zero.

15. Eric Shawn, James Rosen, " Ground Zero mosque Developers Deny Talk of Relocation," FoxNews.com, August 18, 2010, http://www.foxnews.com/politics/2010/08/17/ny-governor-meet-nyc-mosque-developers/.

16. Raheel Raza and Tarek Fatah, "Mischief in Manhattan," *Ottawa Citizen*, August 9, 2010, http://www.ottawacitizen.com/sports/Mischief+Manhattan/3370303/story.html.

17. Mark Impomeni, "Mosque Moves Forward, Yet Church in Limbo," *Human Events*, August 9, 2010, http://www.humanevents.com/article.php?id=38462.

18. Thomas Sowell, "An Old Newness," *National Review*, April 29, 2008, retrieved at http://article.nationalreview.com/?q=MzA2OGM1MjU5YmZmMzc4MGI5NGU4Yzg0YTk1Y2ZhMWI=&w=MQ==.

19. Jim Downey, "CNN Univision Democratic Debate" parody, *Saturday Night Live*, NBC Television, February 23, 2008, http://snltranscripts.jt.org/07/07edebate.phtml.

20. John Zogby, "Zogby Poll: Almost No Obama Voters Ace Election Test," Zogby.com, November 18, 2008, http://www.zogby.com/news/ReadNews.cfm?ID=1642.

21. Brittany Farrell, "An Enlightened Citizenry," Family North Carolina Magazine, Summer 2010, http://www.ncfpc.org/FNC/1007atissue.html.

22. Quoted by Ted Brader, *Campaigning For Hearts and Minds* (Chicago: University of Chicago press, 2006), 109.

23. President John F. Kennedy, Inaugural Address, January 20, 1961, *Inaugural Addresses of the Presidents of the United States* (Washington, D.C.: U.S. Government Printing Office, 1989), www.bartleby.com/124/.

24. John Stossel, "A Duty Not To Vote?," Townhall.com, October 29, 2008, retrieved at http://townhall.com/columnists/JohnStossel/2008/10/29/a_duty_not_to_vote.

25. President John F. Kennedy, "Remarks in Nashville at the 90th Anniversary Convocation of Vanderbilt University," Nashville, May 18, 1963, John F. Kennedy Presidential Library & Museum, http://www.jfklibrary.org/Historical+Resources/Archives/Reference+Desk/Speeches/JFK/003POF03Vanderbilt05181963.htm.

Chapter Five: Restoring Sanity in the Classroom

1. Dennis Prager, "Compassion and the Decline of America," *Human Events*, March 20, 2007, retrieved at http://www.humanevents.com/article.php?id=19896&keywords=tenure.

2. Benjamin S. Bloom, *All Our Children Learning: A Primer for Parents, Teachers, and Other Educators* (New York: McGraw-Hill, 1981), 180.

3. Ann Wilson, "Outcome Based Education—Questions Demanding Answers," excerpt from *Pavlov's Children: A Study of Performance/Outcome-Based Education*, retrieved at http://www.sntp.net/education/OBE_1.htm.

4. Sam Dillon, "Literacy Falls for Graduates From College, Testing Finds," *The New York Times*, December 16, 2005, http://www.nytimes.com/2005/12/16/education/16literacy.html?_r=1&scp=1&sq=Sam%20Dillon%20literacy&st=cse&oref=slogin.

5. Benjamin Samuel Bloom, David R. Krathwohl, Bertran B. Masia, *Taxonomy of Educational Objectives: The Classification of Educational Goals* (London: Longman, 1964), 54.

6. Bloom, et al, ibid., 91.

7. Charlotte Iserbyt, *The Deliberate Dumbing Down of America* (Ravenna, OH: Conscience Press, 1999), text retrieved at http://www.deliberatedumbingdown.com/MomsPDFs/DDDoA.sml.pdf.

8. Ibid.

9. Ibid.

10. Kathryn Ecclestone and Dennis Hayes, *The Dangerous Rise of Therapeutic Education: How Teaching is Becoming Therapy* (New York: Routledge, 2009), 31.

11. Ibid.

12. Alexandra Frean, "Emphasis on Emotions Creates 'Can't Do' Students," *The Times* of London, June 12, 2008, retrieved at http://www.timesonline.co.uk/tol/life_and_style/education/article4116531.ece.

13. Ecclestone and Hayes, ibid., 42.

14. U.S. Supreme Court, "*Engel V. Vitale*, 370 U.S. 421 (1962)," retrieved at http://laws.findlaw.com/us/370/421.html.

15. Justice Antonin Scalia, Dissenting Opinion, "Mccreary County v. American Civil Liberties Union of Kentucky," (03-1693) 545 U.S. 844 (2005), 354 F.3d 438, affirmed, Supreme Court Collection, Cornell University Law School, retrieved at http://www.law.cornell.edu/supct/html/03-1693.ZD.html.

16. World Net Daily, "Judicial Jihad: Judge Rules Islamic Education OK in California Classrooms," WorldNetDaily.com, December 13, 2003, retrieved at http://www.wnd.com/news/article.asp?ARTICLE_ID=36118; Vicki Haddock, "A School Lesson on 'Jihad'," *The San Francisco Chronicle*, September 8, 2002, retrieved at http://www.sfgate.com/cgi-bin/article.cgi?f=/c/a/2002/09/08/IN87674.DTL; Newsmax, "Same Judge OK'ed Muslim Prayer," Newsmax.com, June 1, 2004, retrieved at http://archive.newsmax.com/archives/ic/2004/6/1/230708.shtml.

17. Art Moore, "Feds Arrest Leading Muslim Activist," WorldNetDaily.com, September 29, 2003, retrieved at http://www.worldnetdaily.com/news/article.asp?ARTICLE_ID=34834; Bob Unruh Why Johnny is reading Islamist propaganda: Critics charge Muslim radicals determining textbook content," WorldNetDaily.com, October 26, 2006, retrieved at http://www.worldnetdaily.com/news/article.asp?ARTICLE_ID=52623; Christopher Dickey, "K Is for Vendetta: Why does the Bush administration want to believe that Kaddafi has changed his ways?," Newsweek Web Exclusive, May 17, 2006, retrieved at http://www.newsweek.com/id/47791.

18. Quoted by Mordechai Steinman with Dr. Gerald Schroeder, "The Fine Tuning of the Universe," ScienceFindsGod.com, January 10, 2006, retrieved at http://www.sciencefindsgod.com/blog/2006/01/fine-tuning-of-universe.html.

19. Maynard Smith, J. & Szathmáry, E., "On the Likelihood of Habitable Worlds," Nature, Vol. 384, No. 14, November 14, 1996, p.107.

20. Darrel R. Falk, Coming to Peace With Science: Bridging the Worlds Between Faith and Biology (Downers Grove, IL: InterVarsity Press, 2004), 56.

21. John Frederic Kilner, Paige Comstock Cunningham, and W. David Hager, editors, The Reproduction Revolution (Grand Rapids: Wm. B. Eerdmans Publishing, 2000), 223.

22. Bob Egelko, Jill Tucker, " Homeschoolers' Setback Sends Shock Waves through State," The San Francisco Chronicle, March 7, 2008, retrieved at http://www.sfgate.com/cgi-bin/article.cgi?f=/c/a/2008/03/07/MNJDVF0F1.DTL.

23. Hans Zeiger, "Confusion In Our Schools: Attacks on Home Schooling Ignore the Real Problem," The Hillsdale Collegian (Michigan), October 23, 2003, retrieved at http://www.hillsdalesites.org/collegian/127/127_06/opinions/opinions102303homeschooling.htm.

24. Quoted by Mathew D. Staver, Eternal Vigilance (Nashville: B&H Publishing Group, 2005), 10.

25. Stefan Merrill Block, "Happy, Involved, Well-Adjusted and (!) Home Schooled," *The Cleveland Plain Dealer*, May 28, 2008, retrieved at http://www.cleveland.com/news/plaindealer/othercolumns/index.ssf?/base/opinion/1211963555112130.xml&coll=2&thispage=1.

26. Michael Smith, "Home-Schooling: California Court Reverses Decision," *The Washington Times*, September 7, 2008, retrieved at http://washingtontimes.com/news/2008/sep/07/california-court-reverses-decision/.

27. C.S. Lewis, *The Complete C.S. Lewis Signature Classics* (New York: HarperOne, 2007), pp. 293-294.

Chapter Six: Restoring Sanity in the Family

1. Pat Williams, *Souls of Steel: How to Build Character in Ourselves and Our Kids* (Nashville: FaithWords, 2008), pp. 50-51.

2. Rodney Clapp, *A Peculiar People* (Downers Grove, IL: InterVaristy Press, 1996), 176.

3. George Barna, "Americans Are Most Likely to Base Truth on Feelings," Barna Research Group, February 12, 2002, retrieved at http://www.barna.org/FlexPage.aspx?Page=BarnaUpdate&BarnaUpdateID=106.

4. Ibid.

5. Gil Reavill, *Smut: A Sex-Industry Insider (and Concerned Father) Says Enough is Enough* (New York: Penguin, 2005), pp. 24-25.

6. Ibid., 20.

7. Ibid., 10.

8. Amy Frykholm, "Addictive Behavior: Pastors And Pornography," *The Christian Century*, September 4, 2007, retrieved at http://www.christiancentury.org/article.lasso?id=3629.

9. Chuck Colson "Sexual Ethics: The Victims of Porn," BreakPoint Commentaries, October 29, 2007, retrieved at http://www.breakpoint.org/listingarticle.asp?ID=7175.

10. Ibid.

11. Staff, "Virtually Home Alone: Why Don't Parents Control Their Kids' Media Consumption?" *The Wall Street Journal*, March 11, 2005, retrieved at http://www.opinionjournal.com/taste/?id=110006401.

12. CBS News, "Mom Feared Teen Was 'Boy Crazy,'" CBSNews. com, November 14, 2005, retrieved at http://www.cbsnews.com/ stories/2005/11/14/earlyshow/main1041523.shtml; MSNBC, When Murder Hits The Blogosphere: Personal Sites Suddenly Very Public in Aftermath of Pennsylvania Killing," MSNBC.com, December 1, 2005, retrieved at http://www.msnbc.msn.com/id/10272868/; Fox News Channel, "Pennsylvania Teen Pleads Guilty to Killing Girlfriend's Parents, Gets Life in Prison," FoxNews.com, June 14, 2006, retrieved at http://www.foxnews.com/story/0,2933,199468,00.html.

Chapter Seven: Restoring Sanity in the Church
1. Christopher Landau, "Interview with The Archbishop of Canterbury, Dr Rowan Williams," broadcast on *The World at One*, February 7, 2008, BBC Radio 4, retrieved at http://www.bbc.co.uk/radio4/news/wato/ archbishoptranscript.shtml; Jonathan Petre, Andrew Porter, "Archbishop Williams Sparks Sharia Law Row," *The Telegraph* (UK), February 8, 2008, retrieved at http://www.telegraph.co.uk/news/uknews/1577928/ Archbishop-Williams-sparks-sharia-law-row.html.
2. Riazat Butt, "Uproar as Archbishop Says Sharia Law Inevitable in UK," *The Guardian*, February 8, 2008, retrieved at http://www.guardian. co.uk/politics/2008/feb/08/uk.religion.
3. Charles Colson, "Worldview: The Archbishop and Sharia; What Empty Churches Are Made of," BreakPoint Commentaries, February 25, 2008, retrieved at http://www.breakpoint.org/listingarticle.asp?ID=7579.
4. Abul Taher, " Revealed: UK's First Official Sharia Courts," *The Sunday Times* (of London), September 14, 2008, retrieved at http://www. timesonline.co.uk/tol/news/uk/crime/article4749183.ece.
5. A. Millar, "This Sceptered Isle: From Magna Carta to Sharia Law— Britain's Decline," *The Brussels Journal*, September 15, 2008, retrieved at http://www.brusselsjournal.com/node/3522/print.
6. Maxim Lott, "Advocates of Anti-Shariah Measures Alarmed by Judge's Ruling," August 5, 2010, FoxNews.com, http://www.foxnews.com/ us/2010/08/05/advocates-anti-shariah-measures-alarmed-judges-ruling/.

7. C. S. Lewis, *Mere Christianity* (New York: HarperCollins, 2001), 140.

8. You can explore the evidence for the Christian faith in such books as C. S. Lewis' *Mere Christianity*, *The Case for Faith* and *The Case for Christ* by Lee Strobel, *When Skeptics Ask* and *I Don't Have Enough Faith to Be an Atheist* by Norman L. Geisler, *Hard Questions, Real Answers* by William Lane Craig, *Who Made God? and Answers to Over 100 Other Tough Questions of Faith* by Ravi Zacharias, and *The Apologetics Study Bible: Understand Why You Believe* by Charles Colson.

9. Quoted by Carl N. Degler, *Out of Our Past: The Forces that Shaped Modern America* (New York: HarperCollins, 1983), 18.

10. Canon Dyson Hague, "The History of the Higher Criticism," originally published in 1910, retrieved at http://www.xmission.com/~fidelis/volume1/chapter1/hague.php.

11. Nancy Pearcey, *Total Truth: Liberating Christianity from Its Cultural Captivity* (Wheaton,IL: Good News Publishers, 2005), 291.

12. Mark Steyn, *America Alone: The End of the World as We Know It*, (Washington, DC: Regnery, 2006), 96.

13. Charles Colson, "Religion & Society: Oprahfication and Its Discontents— Our Mile-Wide, Inch-Deep Religious Culture," BreakPoint Commentaries, April 8, 2002, retrieved at http://www.breakpoint.org/listingarticle.asp?ID=4174.

14. David Van Biema, "Christians: No One Path to Salvation," *Time Magazine*, June 23, 2008, retrieved by http://www.time.com/time/nation/article/0,8599,1817217,00.html?xid=feed-yahoo-full-nation.

15. Charles Colson, ibid.

16. The Layman staff, "Church Removes Crosses and Covers up Windows to Accommodate Islamic School," *The Layman* Online, May 26, 2004, http://www.layman.org/news.aspx?article=14652.

17. Megan Hart, "Spring Lake's Christ Community Church Removes Cross, Changes Name to C3Exchange," *The Muskegon Chronicle*, June 23, 2010, http://www.mlive.com/news/muskegon/index.ssf/2010/06/spring_lakes_christ_community.html; Andrew Zarowny, "Church Removes Cross To Appease Non-Christians & Progressives," RightPundits.com, June 27, 2010, http://www.rightpundits.com/?p=6494.

18. Steve Chalke, "Redeeming the Cross: The Lost Message of Jesus & the Cross of Christ," 2004, http://adrianwarnock.com/chalkeoncross.pdf.

19. M.H. Shakir, translator, *The Holy Qur'an* (Elmhurst, NY: Tahrike Tarsile Qur'an, 1999), http://www.usc.edu/schools/college/crcc/engagement/resources/texts/muslim/quran/004.qmt.html.

20. R. C. Sproul, "Burning Hearts Are Not Nourished by Empty Heads," *Christianity Today*, September 3, 1982, 100.

21. Os Guinness, *Fit Bodies, Fat Minds: Why Evangelicals Don't Think and What to Do about It* (Grand Rapids, MI: Baker Books, 1994), pp. 9, 10-11.

Chapter Eight: Agents of Sanity in a World Gone Mad

1. Mahmoud Ahmadinejad, President of Iran, "Full text of President Ahmadinejad's Speech at General Assembly," United Nations, New York, September 17, 2005, IRNA—Islamic Republic News Agency, retrieved at http://www.globalsecurity.org/wmd/library/news/iran/2005/iran-050918-irna02.htm.

2. Dore Gold, *The Fight for Jerusalem: Radical Islam, the West, and the Future of the Holy City* (Washington, DC: Regnery, 2007), pp. 231-233; "Mahdī," *Encyclopædia Britannica* (Encyclopædia Britannica Online), retrieved at http://www.britannica.com/EBchecked/topic/358096/mahdi.

3. Joseph Farah, "Iran President: Terrorist, Murderer, Yet, Bush Says U.S. Will Permit Him to Visit UN," WorldNetDaily.com, August 31, 2005, retrieved at http://www.worldnetdaily.com/news/article.asp?ARTICLE_ID=46060.

4. Dore Gold, ibid., 232.

5. Wendy Kaminer, *Sleeping With Extraterrestrials: The Rise of Irrationalism and Perils of Piety* (New York: Vintage, 2000), 4.

6. Ravi Zacharias, Address to the United Nations' Prayer Breakfast, October 30, 2007, retrieved at http://www.rzim.org/GlobalElements/GFV/tabid/449/ArticleID/96/CBModuleId/1045/Default.aspx.

7. Joe Garofoli, "Evangelical Teens Rally in S.F.," *San Francisco Chronicle*, March 25, 2006, A1.

8. Kevin Libin, "So How Did 'An Inconvenient Truth' Become Required Classroom Viewing?," *National Post* (Canada), May 19, 2007, retrieved at http://www.nationalpost.com/news/story.html?id=f7806f79-bf1f-4bd1-8d33-c904feb71047.

9. Randy Hall, "College Students in Rhode Island Must Watch 'Inconvenient Truth' to Graduate," Cybercast News Service, May 11, 2007, retrieved at http://www.crosswalk.com/news/religiontoday/11540191/; Steven Milloy, "Junk Science: Climate-Controlled Classroom?," Fox News Channel, May 10, 2007, retrieved at http://www.foxnews.com/story/0,2933,271256,00. html.

10. Kevin Libin, ibid.

11. David Adam, "Gore's Climate Film Has Scientific Errors—Judge," *The Guardian* (United Kingdom), October 11, 2007, retrieved at http://www.guardian.co.uk/environment/2007/oct/11/ climatechange?gusrc=rss&feed=8.

12. Author uncredited, "Global Warming Worries," GMTV (Good Morning Television, UK), March 19, 2007, retrieved at http://www.gm.tv/index. cfm?articleid=24717.

13. Bob Unruh, "Heat of the Moment: 31,000 Scientists Reject 'Global Warming' Agenda," WorldNetDaily.com, May 19, 2008, retrieved at http:// www.worldnetdaily.com/index.php?fa=PAGE.view&pageId=64734.

14. Charles Colson, "Thirty Pints of Blood," BreakPoint Commentaries, March 6, 2007, retrieved at http://www.breakpoint.org/listingarticle. asp?ID=6236; Robert Bazell, "A human life is a human life: At U.S. military field hospitals, care and compassion for wounded enemies," NBC News, March 2, 2007 retrieved at http://www.msnbc.msn.com/id/17406009/.

Epilogue

1. David M. Walker, *Comeback America: Turning the Country Around and Restoring Fiscal Responsibility* (New York: Random House, 2009), 36-37.

2. Niall Ferguson, "Complexity and Collapse: Empires on the Edge of Chaos," Foreign Affairs, Published by the Council on Foreign

Relations, March/April 2010, http://www.foreignaffairs.com/
articles/65987/niall-ferguson/complexity-and-collapse.

3. Will Durant, *Caesar and Christ*, "Epilogue" (New York: Simon &
Schuster, 1980), 665.

4. Charles Krauthammer, "Decline Is a Choice: The New
Liberalism and the End of American Ascendancy," 2009
Wriston Lecture at the Manhattan Institute for Policy Research,
October 5, 2009, published in *The Weekly Standard*, October
19, 2009, http://www.weeklystandard.com/Content/Public/
Articles/000/000/017/056lfnpr.asp

About the Author

Dr. Michael Youssef was born in Egypt and moved to Australia, where he studied at Moore Theological College in Sydney and was ordained to the ministry. He and his wife Elizabeth came to America in 1977, and he received a Master's in Theology from Fuller Theological Seminary. He also earned a doctorate in social anthropology from Emory University in Atlanta. Dr. Youssef became a United States citizen in 1984.

In 1987, Dr. Youssef founded The Church of the Apostles in Atlanta with fewer than 40 adults. It has since grown to a congregation of over 3,000. The church also serves as the launching pad for the international radio, television, print, and Internet ministry of *Leading The Way*, an organization that broadcasts Bible teaching in 20 languages to more than 200 countries. He is the author of more than two-dozen books, the latest being *The Greatest Lie*.

Follow Dr. Youssef on twitter @michaelayoussef and through his news blog www.michaelyoussef.com